Key Concepts in Chinese Thought and Culture

Published in partnership between FLTRP and Palgrave Macmillan, the Key Concepts in Chinese Thought and Culture offer a unique insight into Chinese culture, defining and contextualizing some of China's most fundamental and at times complex philosophical concepts. In a concise and reader-friendly manner, these works define a variety of quintessentially Chinese terms such as harmony (hé/和) or association (xīng/兴) – and examine how they first appeared and developed in Chinese culture, the impact they had on Chinese thought and why they continue to have significant meaning in China today. At a time when the understanding of different histories, languages and cultures globally is at a premium, this series provides a valuable roadmap to the concepts which underpin 21st century Chinese society.

Dejia Li

Conceptual History of Morality and Penalty in China

中华思想文化术语传播工程
Key Concepts in Chinese Thought and Culture: Communication Through Translation

palgrave macmillan

Dejia Li
Beijing, China

Translated by
Linan Tian
Beijing, China

ISSN 2524-8464 ISSN 2524-8472 (electronic)
Key Concepts in Chinese Thought and Culture
ISBN 978-981-95-9058-2 ISBN 978-981-95-9059-9 (eBook)
https://doi.org/10.1007/978-981-95-9059-9

Jointly published with Foreign Language Teaching and Research Publishing Co., Ltd
The print edition is not for sale in China (Mainland). Customers from China (Mainland) please order the print book from: Foreign Language Teaching and Research Publishing Co., Ltd.

This Palgrave Macmillan imprint is published by the registered company Springer Nature Singapore Pte Ltd.
The registered company address is: 152 Beach Road, #21-01/04 Gateway East, Singapore 189721, Singapore

Contents

CHAPTER 1

De(Virtue) and Xing(Penalty): Interpretation of the Two Ancient Concepts

1 Origin and Development of "De" in Ancient China

Earlier scholarship treated "De" as no more than morality or moral edification, overlooking its function as a criterion of political legitimacy in the pre-Qin period (before 221BCE) and its intrinsic nexus with institution-construction. Moreover, it was seldom recognized that the opposition between "De" and "Xing" in ancient China was not merely a difference between two ruling models, but a distinction between two political modes and social governance forms. The original meaning of "De" was undoubtedly related to morality, and its earliest extended meaning was also associated with goodness and virtue. However, "De" in ancient China was more than morality and virtue; instead, it was a complex and abstract concept with rich philosophical connotations. After King Wu (Ji Fa) conquered the Shang Dynasty (1600-1046BCE) and established Zhou Dynasty (1046BC-256BCE), people of Zhou changed their primitive understanding of "De". For the first time, people interpreted "De" from the perspectives of political legitimacy, enriching its connotation. In Western Zhou period, the Confucian scholars inherited the important value of "De", setting the basic connotation of "De" in ancient China.

D. Li, *Conceptual History of Morality and Penalty in China*, Key Concepts in Chinese Thought and Culture,
https://doi.org/10.1007/978-981-95-9059-9_1

I. The Origin of "De"

The emergence of the concept "De(virtue/morality)" was closely linked to the rise of "private property". In primitive times, property was held in common, with no clear distinctions among individuals; thus, there was neither the awareness of private property nor the concept of "De". Xia, Shang, and Zhou Dynasties (2070-256BCE) had always been praised in historical records, as people served for the benefit of society as a whole and selected the virtuous and capable as rulers. However, such selflessness was manifesting the absence of "private property". While selflessness was certainly a virtue yearned for by later generations, it indeed had not been possessed by people at that time, even not in the Xia Dynasty (2070BC-1600BC), according to existing historical materials.

Nowadays, scholars often trace the origin of "De" back to the Shang Dynasty (1600-1046BC). From the inscriptions on bones or tortoise shells and records in *The Book of History · Pangeng*, it is evident that people of Shang Dynasty had already developed the concept of "De". Some scholars argue that in the Shang Dynasty, "De" was associated with warfare, property, and sacrifices, and had not yet carried the implications of morality or virtue [1]. Based on the scholarly research and existing historical documents, the concept of "De" held by the people in Shang Dynasty can be characterized by the following three aspects.

First, according to the inscriptions on bones or tortoise shells, Shang people often interpreted "De" as obtaining or gaining something, based on which, Wu Shuchen discussed the connection between "De" in Shang oracle bone inscriptions and elements such as property, warfare, and sacrifices, arguing that the concept of "De" in Shang Dynasty originated from property exchange or military conquest [1]. Such understanding of "De" can also be corroborated by later exegetical works. For example, in *The Book of Rite · Yueji*, here states, De is that which is obtained.

Second, the form of "德" ("De" we discussing here in Chinese character) in oracle bone inscriptions is a pictograph combining "彳" (representing movement or action) and "直" (meaning straight or direct). Mr. Xu Zhongshu believed that "直" resembles the shape of an eye hanging straight to seek uprightness, and "彳" conveys the meaning of "walking" or "moving". Thus, the character "德(De)" should be interpreted as following a path and observing carefully [2]. Compared with the character "悳" (a variant of "De") in bronze inscriptions, "De" in inscriptions on bones or tortoise shells lacks the "心" ("heart") radical, while consists of the radicals representing "movement" and "horizontal eye", meaning to look around on the road or to walk along a path. This indicates at that time, "De" had not yet been internalized as morality. In addition, the form of "De" in bone script (combining "movement" and "horizontal eye") paved way for endowing "De" with morality-related connotations. With the meanings of "abide by", "comply with", and "follow" implied in the inscriptions on bones or tortoise shells, "De" can be interpreted as the reverence of human rulers to ancestors or gods, which means the rulers should act and govern in accordance with the indications of ancestors and gods.

Third, "De" of the Shang people was a concept opposite to punishment. Two examples from *The Book of History · Pangeng* can illustrate this:

> I will notimpose improper punishments on you. Similarly, I will notgrant you improper favors.
> Regardless of kinship or distance, I will mete out punishments according to your crimes, and I will also bestow rewards based on your merits [3].

In short, these two passages clearly indicate that "De" and punishment are defined in opposition to each other. For those subjected to punishment, it entails a form of loss. In contrast, "De" can be interpreted to its extended sense as "favor" or "benefit" [4].

In summary, the core meaning of "De" in the Shang Dynasty is "obtaining", referring to receiving care and grace from the Mandate of Heaven and Ancestors. In the worldview of the Shang people, the two concepts were not distinguished; Ancestor was the representative of Heaven, linking Heaven and humans. In Shang Dynasty, "De" was also an expression of the Mandate of Heaven. When people praised "De", they were praising the gifts from Heaven and ancestors. "De" possessed by the kings was also attributed to the endowment of the Mandate of Heaven and the protection of ancestors. Due to such belief, the tyrannical King Dixin (the last king of Shang Dynasty) refused to reform and rejected the admonishment from virtuous ministers. His statement, "my life is not secured by the decree of Heaven" [5] is a true reflection of how the tyrant, believe himself to be the beneficiary of the Mandate of Heaven and act without fear. Throughout the entire Shang Dynasty, the understanding of "De" was overshadowed by the Mandate of Heaven, failing to separate from the concept of divine will and develop into a rationalized and secularized political view.

II. De in Zhou Dynasty

During the transitional period between the Shang and Zhou Dynasties, the entire society had witnessed tremendous changes on values, ideology, culture, and political structure. Wang Guowei commented on this upheaval that no transformation in politics and culture in China was more drastic than that [6]. Stemmed from Zhou people's skepticism toward "the Mandate of Heaven" prevailed in Shang Dynasty, the ideological upheaval manifested the weakening of "the Mandate of Heaven" and the emphasis on "De". In Zhou Dynasty, people began to contemplate the relationship between the Mandate of Heaven and the human king. Since the Shang Dynasty was replaced by the Zhou, it proved that the Mandate of Heaven was transferable. Then, how can a regime retain the Mandate of Heaven and receive the favor? This reflection is regarded by modern observers as an inquiry into and reflection on the source of political legitimacy. People in Zhou Dynasty believed that the Mandate of Heaven was not permanent, and only those with "De" would be favored by Heaven. Only those who love people and care for the well-being of people could be endowed "De" and further gain the favor from the Mandate of Heaven [7].

At the beginning of the Zhou Dynasty, the connotation of "De" inherited while also developed and changed certain aspects of the Shang understanding of "De". It continued Shang tradition of obeying heaven as the highest deity while carried the meaning of obtaining, like, obtaining the Mandate of Heaven, which rationalized and secularized the purely theocratic concept of "De" in Shang Dynasty, transforming it into a human-related issue rather other purely defined by Heaven. "De" in Zhou Dynasty shifted from mere focus on the Mandate of Heaven and divine will to concern for humans and reflection on the gains and losses of governance, marking a great development in the history of Chinese thought.

"De" in Zhou Dynasty was not limited to the meaning of morality or virtue but contained rich connotations, among which the most important was the reflection on political virtue or legitimacy. Regarding political legitimacy, its core lay in applying morality-based standards and expectations to actual political practice. In essence, it constituted a moral judgment. Such moral judgment is not necessarily the preserve to a rule by man society; on the contrary, a rule of law society even more requires morality as a higher norm to judge whether the politics is justified. In the Zhou Dynasty, "De" was the norm for judging the legitimacy of politics at the time.

Based on this, the rich connotations of "De" in Zhou Dynasty can be explored from the following three aspects:

1. The relationship between "De" and governance related to Mandate of Heaven. First of all, "De" provided a legitimate basis for regime. In Zhou Dynasty, people regarded "De" as the foundation for the Mandate of Heaven. Interpreted through the framework of modern political discourse, this means that the Zhou people took "De" as the basis for judging whether the regime was legitimate and justified. If the ruler himself was endowed with "De" and governed following the doctrine of "De", such regime would be blessed by Heaven and thus be legitimate. Secondly, "De" was reflected in the way of governance. "De" was taken as the standard for handling governance affairs in Zhou Dynasty, which paved way for rule by virtue and benevolent governance in subsequent generations.
2. The relationship between "De" and the feudal system. In the Zhou Dynasty, the political system was constructed based on the standards of "De", internalizing "De" as the inherent requirement of the national political system. Wang Guowei was the first scholar to realize the close connection between "De" and the feudal system. In his famous work, *On the Systems of the Shang and Zhou Dynasties*, he pointed out that the major institutional reforms in the Zhou Dynasty were the rising of feudal patriarchal, ancestral temple, and prohibition of marriage within the same surname [8]. In his view, the institutions in Zhou Dynasty and "De" were intertwined: the institutions embodied "De", while "De" in turn regulated the institutions, resulting in a unified and integrated system. The relationship between "De" in the Western Zhou Dynasty and its institutional system is reflected in selecting those with virtue

and establishing the country through patriarchal and enfeoffment system, which were the foundation of the Zhou Dynasty Both enfeoffment and patriarchal were closely related to "De", and ran with "De" as the standard, incorporating nobles of all ranks and even ordinary people into this system. Every class and individual in Zhou lived under the direction of "De", respecting the king and clan leaders, and being content with their position without rebellious intentions. This was the important connotation of "De" in the institution of Western Zhou Dynasty. "De" in Zhou Dynasty not only provided a legitimate foundation of obeying Heaven and caring the well-being of people but also indicated that the stable order of people's lives was originated from the patriarchal clan and enfeoffment system, and from the deliberate design and arrangement of institutional "De".

3. The relationship between "De" and "inspection". Based on the definition of "hegemon(Ba)" in *Zuo's Commentary on The Spring and Autumn Annals*, Ogura Yoshihiko studied the evolution of "De" in ancient China. Ogura Yoshihiko believed that "De" was related to the character "省 (inspect)" in bronze inscriptions, which had three meanings: (1) inspection of regions (Sheng Fang); (2) hunting (Sheng Tian); (3) conquest. Ogura Yoshihiko argued that the king inspected to urge tribute payment, resorting to military action in cases of defiance, and permitting autonomy when submission was shown, which precisely practiced the principle of hegemon, integrating virtue and punishment, mentioned in *Zuo's Commentary on The Spring and Autumn Annals* [9]. The Zhou king's inspection of the subordinated feudal states was a demonstration of political power and a display of military strength. As a way to declare political power, "Sheng Fang" implied conquering those who refused to submit, and controlling over the states through political and military actions. If we take "Sheng Fang" as a conciliatory political strategy, the guarantee to running it was military conquest backed by state violence. The dual strategies of gentleness and force—embodied respectively in the inspection of the regions and punitive expeditions—were two important political strategies for the Zhou people to expand their territory and stabilize the country. Acting with proper relaxation and tension of these two manners had always been the principle of governance. Tracing back to the source, such

balance was originated from "Sheng Fang" and "conquest" during the Shang and Zhou Dynasties.

As mentioned earlier, "Sheng Fang" in bone inscriptions had a certain origin with the character "De". As a conciliatory politics, "Sheng Fang" was also culturally related to "De" in the Shang and Zhou Dynasties.

Firstly, the "Sheng Fang" institution reflected the Zhou king's political purpose of educating the people with virtue. *The Book of Changes* interpreted "Sheng Fang" as a way for the Zhou king to observe folk customs and offer them civilization, which indicated that this institution not only had the function of demonstrating military and political power but also had the implication of inspecting social education. Secondly, "Sheng Fang", which implied tour-inspection and conquest, reflected the Zhou people's political strategy of combining hardness and softness, and balancing civil and military governance. This reflects the ancient principle of "mollifying the central states with virtue and awing the barbarians of the four quarters with punishment". Bestowing kindness on the common people to gain their obedience, while conquering and suppressing those who refused to accept the emperor's kindness, with the strategy combining hardness and softness, the governance could both resort to force at any time and seek the potential of turning war into peace.

2 Origin and Development of "Xing" in Ancient China

A further misunderstanding in the theory of "virtue given priority over penalty" lies in the interpretation of the ancient concept of "Xing". In the past, many scholars equated the concept and connotation of "Fa(law)" in ancient China with the modern Western concept of "law" and held that "Fa" in traditional Chinese society was mostly equivalent to "Xing(punishment)", they further concluded that "Fa" in ancient China indicated penalty or punishment and reward. One of the major conceptual misunderstandings of the "virtue given priority over penalty" theory lies in the conflation of "Xing(penalty)" and "Fa(law)" in ancient society, which has led to a literal misreading of "virtue given priority over penalty" as suggesting that moral education was prioritized while the development of legal systems was neglected. In fact, Yan Fu had already pointed out that there were four translations of "law" in western society, which were Li (reason), Li (rite), Fa (law), and Zhi (institution), and scholars should examine this carefully. He further stated, "The Western concept of 'law' in fact encompasses both Chinese li(rite) and Code" [10]. Therefore, reason, rite, law, penalty, and institution in traditional society each embody certain dimensions of "law" in modern society. However, it would be erroneous to conclude that any of these alone fully represent the comprehensive notion of "law". In fact, "Xing" in ancient China not only indicated penalty or criminal law, but also symbolized a political means corresponding to "De". As mentioned above, "De" and "Xing" were derived from the political systems of "Sheng(De) Fang" and "Xun Shou" (touring and hunting), and they themselves were part of the system.

In contrast to the Confucians, the Legalists supported "Xing" as the basic principle of governance and the model of social management during the Warring States Period. The statement, "people in ancient times were eager for virtue, people in the middle ages pursued wisdom, and people today strive for power", was the reflection of the choice of legalism. The legalism model of rule by penalty, was to unite the national strength to build a centralized autocratic monarchy with penalty and reward as means under the principles of "Yi Xing" (unified the standard of penalty) and "Yi Jiao" (unified people's thought).

I. The Character Meaning and Origin of "Xing"

1. The Character Meaning of "Xing"

In *Analytical Dictionary of Characters*, it states that the character form of "Xing" in ancient China implied a punishment for crimes, and the original character form of "Xing(刑)" was "井(jing)", which, according to modern scholars, had already been used in bronze inscriptions in Western Zhou period. There are three main meanings of "井(jing)" in bronze inscription: (1) it has the meaning of "Xing", including killing, conquering, and punishing, and later its character form gradually developed into the modern version of "刑"; (2) it is used as the name of a place, a person, or a state. For example, "Jing Hou" mentioned in the inscription of *Mai Zun* and "Jing Yi" mentioned in the inscription of *San Pan*; (3) it is conformity to "型 (model)", It means that the relevant authorities shall punish the officials who disrupt politics, fail to follow the models of the former kings, oppress the people, and insult the widows and orphans. The king required Mu(an official title) should also be insightful, upright, and act in accordance with the law. In this context, "Jing" means a model or a paradigm, extended to a criterion or law.

2. "Xing" Arose from War

A prevailing theory regarding the origin of "Xing" is the notion that "punishment arises from war", suggesting that penal sanctions largely emerged during tribal conflicts or were even directly applied in warfare. Ancient scholars once systematically argued this idea. *The History of Liao·Treatise on Punishment* states, punishment arises from war and ends for rites. The compilers of *the History of Liao* lived in an era far removed from the origin of Xing, and the claim that punishment arises from war and ends for rites was merely a bold hypothesis formulated by historians based on historical materials available to them and the prevailing understanding of punishment at the time. *The History of Liao* asserts that punishment did not exist in the early stages of civilization. Armed conflicts among the people initially served only for self-defense, and mutual warfare was merely primitive retributive justice. "Xing(punishment)" originated from the chaos incited by Chi You. To quell the disorder and penalize the instigators, Emperor Yao instituted punishment, leading to the saying, Bo-Yi delivered his statutes to prevent the people from rendering themselves obnoxious to punishment.

From extant historical records, the assertion that punishment arises from war and ends for rites could be proved. *The Book of History·Marquis of Lu on Punishments* also mentioned that punishment was established in response to the disorder caused by Chi You. In ancient times, Chiyou incited rebellion and indiscriminately slaughtered the innocent, creating five cruel punishments as laws to suppress the Miao people who disobeyed his decrees. Upon hearing the grievances of the Miao people, Emperor Yao commanded three ministers to govern the populace, among whom Bo-Yi delivered statutes to prevent the people from rendering themselves obnoxious to punishment. This demonstrates that the emergence of punishment was linked to quelling rebellion and disorder.

The assertion that punishment arises from war and ends for rites was a widely accepted interpretation among the ancients regarding the concept of penalty. In their view, punishment and warfare were originally indistinguishable, the only difference was that one was applied to individuals, the other to the realm at large. "De" and "Xing" were juxtaposed in *Zuo's Commentary on The Spring and Autumn Annals*, clarifying that the purpose of punishment was to subjugate rebels by force: "Attack those who rebel and spare those who submit, govern through virtue and penalty, and balance the gentle and aggressive strategy" [11]. Ogura Yoshihiko points out that *Zuo's Commentary on The Spring and Autumn Annals* presents two opposite principles of hegemony: one balancing virtue and punishment, and the other relying solely through military conquest [12]. It clearly demonstrates that punishment carries the meaning of suppressing rebellion and, like "De", which embodies a conciliatory approach, served as a means for feudal lords to achieve dominance during the Spring and Autumn period.

3. "Xing" Originated from "Li"

"Penalty arises from war" is not the only perspective to learn the origin of "Xing(Penalty)". The connection between punishment and war is just one way to understand the complex connotation of "Xing". From the interpretation of "Xing" in later generations, "Xing" refers to a penalty imposed on crimes. Even if it is interpreted as conquest, such conquest was imposed on countries or tribes that had committed crimes. It is thus evident that there is a close connection between "Xing(penalty)" and "Zui(crime)".

Emergence of the concept of crime and penalty in the legal sense is an inevitable result of historical development after the emergence of classes and states. However, from a sociological perspective, the concept of "crime" had already existed before the emergence of states and classes. In early human societies, crime originated from primitive customs and taboos. In the clan societies of early humanity, clan individuals who had not yet shed their primitive innocence often felt a sense of "guilt" or were deemed "guilty" due to their inappropriate actions. Generally speaking, "guilt" in early human societies might be related to tribal totems or common taboos, and stemmed from violations of them. Although primitive totem worship and various taboos in early times seemed incredible, they subtly exerted a huge impact on the development of human society. Human society had been developing gradually, and forming in a "layered accumulation" way. The incremental developments since early human society have subtly shaped the material and spiritual structures of modern civilization. Following the age of savagery, totem worship and various taboos prevailed among primitive tribes, both of which were intricately linked to later political and legal systems.

Wu Shuchen points out that there is a connection between the early Chinese concept of "Xing(penalty)" and tattooing, which existed as a symbol of taboos. To a certain extent, this connection explains that "crime" and "Xing(penalty)" originated from gender taboos in early times. By examining the etymology of "Xing(penalty)", Wu Shuchen found that the original form of the character "刑(Xing)" is "井(Jing)", and 井(Jing) here should be interpreted as "校", a tool for tattooing in primitive societies. Long before the emergence of "Qing" (the punishment of branding) as a penalty, there had been tattooing for a long time. Tattooing culturally indicated a kind of gender taboo in early human society, and its profound meaning was to remind and restrict incest between parents and children, as well as among siblings. The social function of tattooing was to define the relationship between individuals and others or different groups through specific patterns and symbols, thereby deriving behavioral patterns of individuals toward others and groups. Therefore, tattooing was also an important part of rite in ancient times [13].

3 "Xing (Penalty)" in the Shang and Zhou Dynasties

The origin and evolution of the meaning of "Xing(penalty)" reflect the understanding and evaluation of this character by the ancients during the Shang and Zhou Dynasties, offering a comprehensive insight into the concept of "penalty" in that era. Given that the origins of "penalty" were tied to intertribal warfare and sexual taboos in primitive society, the ancients associated "punishment" with the concepts of "war" and "sin". From war and conquest to the discipline and punishment of crimes, "Xing(penalty)" became something terrifying and cruel in people's minds, so much so that when people talked about that, it would remind them of knives, saws, axes, and battleaxes. After the formation of the state and classes, the concept that "military affairs and penalties are indistinguishable" gradually took on the meaning of penalties and criminal norms, and its role in punishing illegal acts in social governance was highlighted.

People in Han Dynasty (206BC–220AD) summarized the meaning of penalty as, law is for stopping violence through punishment [14]. On the one hand, people abhorred the cruelty of penalty; on the other hand, they had to acknowledge its role in calming chaos in social governance. Therefore, people in ancient China always believed that penalty cannot be abolished even in a flourishing age, nor is it advocated in a flourishing age. In *Book of Han*, it even clearly states that penalty is not to secure governance but to calm the chaos [15]. Such a contradictory cultural psychology of valuing the role of penalty while abhorring its cruelty originated from the concept of "Xing" in Shang and Zhou Dynasties, and it was also the psychological basis of the ancient thought of prudential punishment.

During the Shang and Zhou Dynasties, the concept of "Xing" was significantly connected with "De". On the one hand, the concept of "De" is inherently incorporated in the notion of "Xing". In the Western Zhou Dynasty, people categorized penalty into benevolent punishment and oppressive punishment based on whether it aligned with the principle of "De". On the other hand, prudent punishment also became a crucial manifestation of a ruler's virtue. People in Zhou Dynasty advocated ideas of "demonstration of virtue and cautious use of punishment" and "for the end of punishment is to promote virtue". The former emphasizes two key aspects in governing the people: demonstrating virtue which means ensuring that people may receive care and benefits, and exercising caution in punishment which indicates preventing the people from suffering cruel penalties. The latter principle fully demonstrates that virtue and prudent punishment were two sides of the same coin—only by cautiously wielding the state's punitive power could the political ideal of "demonstrating virtue" be achieved. At the same time, prudent punishment itself was a vital expression of the ruler's virtuous governance.

"De" in King Wen's mind, referred to as elevating, meant to increase and bestow, ensuring that people gained benefits. Specifically, in political practice, it indicated the governance ethics of "valuing the people", "educating the people", and "enriching the people", thereby enabling them to prosper [16]. Prudent punishment not only indicated leniency and caution in penal enforcement but also underscored the role of punishment in sanctioning crimes and misconduct, thereby eliminating social ills. This is the principle of striving to eradicate wrongdoing. Valuing the function of punishment entailed the careful application of punishment, as the rulers of Zhou Dynasty proposed a series of specific measures of prudential punishment, such as: no conviction without evidence, which means one could not be punished for intent alone without actual wrong-doing; dealing with doubtful crimes lightly, distinguishing between unintentional and intentional offenses, differentiating occasional offenders from habitual offenders; exempting the children, elderly, disabled, and mentally impaired from punishment, opposing to extend the punishment of offenders to all their relatives.

The concept that "for the end of punishment is to promote virtue" in Western Zhou Dynasty was a profound summary of the relationship between "De" and "Xing". *Marquis of Lu on Punishments* categorized penalties into "benevolent" and "oppressive", with "De(virtue)" serving as the criterion for distinguishing them. Benevolent punishment was ordained by heaven and originated from the sages' wars to quell chaos, whose purpose was not merely to end disorder but to establish virtue and good conduct. Thus, "the end of punishment is to promote virtue" meant to advance moral governance with punishment. Conversely, oppressive punishment not only failed to foster virtue but instead sowed the seeds of turmoil. People in Zhou Dynasty believed that while "benevolent" and "oppressive" punishments might appear similar in form, their effects were diametrically opposed.

In the view of the Western Zhou legislators, the magistrates of the prison system administered punishment to govern the people and instruct them in the practice of morality. Just punishment could serve to make the people submit to instruction and revere virtue. The purpose of establishing and administering punishment was not to establish personal authority, but to benefit the people, thereby ensuring the enduring Mandate of Heaven without violating Heaven's virtue. Here, "virtue" and "punishment" are not two parallel means of governance. "Virtue" represented the Zhou people's description of benevolent politics, the essential requirement for legitimate rule, and the ideal political goal pursued by Zhou rulers. "Punishment", meanwhile, was one of the means to "demonstrate virtue". Thus, the Zhou legislators declared: We approach punishment with reverence; virtue alone justifies punishment.

4 De (Virtue) and Xing (Penalty) as Two Political Principles

Through an examination of the concept of "De(Virtue)" and "Xing(Penalty)" in the pre-Qin period, it is discovered that the terms cannot be simply reduced to moral standards or penal sanctions. In the past, scholars often interpreted "De" to moral instruction or cultivation, failing to recognize that in pre-Qin period, it also implied political legitimacy. Moreover, scholars overlooked the intrinsic connection between "De" and institutional governance, as well as the fact that the opposition between "De(Virtue)" and "Xing(Penalty)" represented not only differing methods of rule but fundamentally distinct political modes and social governance forms. Since the pre-Qin period, the connotation of "De" had not been limited to moral indoctrination as a means of governance. During the Western Zhou Dynasty, "De" primarily denoted the legitimacy of a regime, presenting an ideal of benevolent governance, in the context of which, "De" and "Xing" were not concepts in the same line. Built upon this, the meaning of "De" was expanded to something related to governance structures supported by Confucian scholars, framing it as a political mode embodying benevolent politics and good governance.

The original meaning of "Xing" was indeed tied to penal sanctions, but through the development of Legalism during the pre-Qin period, the term came to signify more than that and certainly cannot be equated with modern law. People in the Zhou Dynasty treated punishment as an instrument of statecraft—a means of governance centered on penal measures. This differs markedly from later views that regarded virtue and punishment as complementary governance tools [17]. Principles like "demonstration of virtue and cautious use of punishment" or "the end of punishment is to promote virtue" positioned "virtue" as the ultimate objective, with "punishment" serving merely as one of the important means to achieve that. During the Spring and Autumn and Warring States periods, "De(virtue)" symbolized the soft power approaches of conciliatory politics and moral cultivation, while "Xing(penalty)" represented the hard power of disciplinary sanctions and military conquest. Gradually, "Xing(penalty)" emerged as a political principle diametrically opposed to "De(virtue)". Opposite to the governance model centered on "De(virtue)" supported by Confucianism, the Legalists supported the doctrine of "rule by law". If the political mode committed by

Confucian was named rule by virtue, then the corresponding model committed by Legalist could be called rule by penalty, which indicates the two models pursue fundamentally divergent political ends and reflects profound disparities in values and governing philosophies.

As previously discussed, in the Shang and Zhou Dynasty, "De(virtue)" was closely tied to the institutions of "Sheng Fang" (inspection tours) and "Xun Shou" (royal hunts), which incorporated two complementary yet opposite methods: As "soft subjugation" entails compelling those who have not yet submitted to the king's rule to yield through methods that are outwardly gentle yet inwardly resolute—such as deterrence, pacification, cultural assimilation, and moral persuasion. Conversely, "hard subjugation" signifies the military conquest of enemies through campaigns of conquest. Thus, the two political principles of softness and hardness employed in the pre-Qin period correspond mutually with "virtue" and "punishment". Therefore, Tao Xisheng maintained that punishment and virtue share an interdependent yet antagonistic relationship. He stated: "Punishment and virtue are interconnected. Those who disregard the norms handed down by our ancestors must face sanctions. Hence, "enlightened virtue" and "enlightened punishment" are pursued concurrently. Yet virtue and punishment are also opposites. This punishment, which stands in opposition to virtue, reveals the reason for its opposition through its very origins" [18]. However, through an examination of the roots of the two, they are essentially opposite". In texts in Pre-Qin period, particularly in *Zuo's Commentary*, "De(Virtue)" and "Xing(Penalty)", the two unexclusive concepts, had always been emphasized together, as "to attack rebels is punishment, to gently subdue is virtue" [19].

The relationship between "De(Virtue)" and "Xing(Penalty)" in *Zuo's Commentary* possesses two fundamental characteristics:

1. Equal political status—"De(Virtue)" and "Xing(Penalty)" are consistently paired with other governing principles like "rite" and "righteousness" as parallel political doctrines.
2. Opposite function—where "De(Virtue)" operates through "conciliation", "appeasement", and "leniency", pacifying people with gentle power, while "Xing(Penalty)" manifests as "conquest", "suppression", and "deterrence", relying on military force to quell rebellion.

As the text states, “detain the disloyal, spare the submissive—the virtue, as well as the punishment should not run too deep. The obedient cherish virtue; the defiant dread punishment” [20]. Since the Western Zhou Dynasty, rulers has embraced the dual approaches—employing virtue to nurture compliant subjects, and punishment to crush dissent. Together, they formed complementary yet antithetical mechanisms for maintaining political order.

Before the rise of Confucianism and Legalism, “carrot-and-stick” had been the mainstream political philosophy. “De(virtue)” governed the obedient through moral suasion, while “Xing(penalty)” violently subdued rebels. “If rebels go unpunished, how can we demonstrate our might; if the compliant receive no mercy, how can we showcase our grace; without both might and grace, how to demonstrate virtue; without virtue, how to claim leadership” [21]. Ogura Yoshihiko identifies this as the “twin principles” or “virtue-punishment dualism” [22]. He traces their origins to “Sheng Fang”, a practice combined “leniency” and “severity”, alternating between military displays and cultural assimilation (what Confucians later called “subduing through virtue”). This demonstrates that the political ideology and principles embodied in the Spring and Autumn period’s discourse on “virtue and punishment” actually bear a clear lineage to the “provincial inspection” system of the Yin-Zhou transition. “‘De(virtue)’ originally linked to ‘Sheng’, serving as a conceptual framework for concrete actions; touring territories to levy grain and troops, escalating to conquest when resisted, and granting clemency upon surrender; such governance model, traceable to late Shang Dynasty, remained key to feudal expansion until mid-Spring and Autumn period”, concluded by Ogura Yoshihiko [23]. Thus, “De(virtue)” and “Xing(penalty)” in Spring and Autumn period were evolved from the two facets of “Sheng Fang”, with “virtue” institutionalizing the pacification strand, reflecting political sophistication, while “punishment” systematizing coercive enforcement as an indispensable tool for sustaining social order.

Since the Spring and Autumn period, “softness” and “De(virtue)” had represented a comprehensive governing principle to be applied in both internal and external affairs. *The Book of History · Hong Fan* mentioned the “Three Virtues” required of rulers: Uprightness, Mastery through Firmness and Mastery through Softness [24]. Zheng Xuan comments that, “mastery” denoting the capability to be firm yet capable of softness, soft yet capable of firmness—balancing leniency and severity to achieve governance and merit [25]. Here, “firmness” and “softness” should be understood in the context of governance. In times of stability, straighten societal distortions through rectitude. Responding to harmony, employ gentle governance to maintain cohesion.

The Book of Changes analogizes such strategy via the dynamics of yin-yang and heaven-earth, stating that proper softness enables cultural supremacy; proper firmness ensures stability [26]. This captures their dialectical relationship as "the earth's essence is supremely soft, yet its movements show firmness". "Punishment" inherits the "firm" aspect, while "virtue" embodies the "soft" principle. In pre-Qin period, both Daoism and Confucianism emphasized "softness", albeit differently. Confucians etymologically tied their identity to softness. As *Writings of Argument and Persuasion* states, 儒 (the character of Confucian) means soft, and it is also be used to name the scholars in ancient China. Grounded in "following nature", Lao Tzu promotes "embracing femininity" [27], which is passive, advising rulers to be "soft" to achieve "non-action governance". The "softness" here indicates political abstinence—avoiding interstate conflicts and refraining from exploiting the people. Compared with this, Confucianism advocates balanced firmness-softness integration. As the saying goes, heaven's way pairs yin-yang, earth's way couples firm-soft; humanity's way joins benevolence-righteousness. Confucius particularly praised the "Northern Strength" of "teaching through gentle tolerance, not retaliating against cruelty"—a model of virtuous governance [28]. Zhang Taiyan interpreted the "softness" as "civilization"—the process of "tempering firmness into softness" through moral education, which reveals the intrinsic linkage between virtue and softness, employing ethical instruction to cultivate pliancy. When Confucius advocated "balancing leniency and severity", he essentially prescribed the integrated application of "De(virtue)" and "Xing(penalty)" in statecraft.

In addition to juxtaposing "De(virtue)" with "Xing(penalty)" or "firmness" with "softness", the contrast between "De(virtue)" and "martial force" had emerged in texts in Spring and Autumn period. As *Yi Zhou Shu* states, to guide the people through their faults is virtue; to brave hardships for them is martial force [29]. The "virtue and martial force" here closely parallels the "virtue and punishment". The adage "virtue softens the central states, punishment awes the border tribes" essentially frames "De(virtue)" as symbolic of cultural governance and "Xing(penalty)" as emblematic of military conquest. Such couplings indicate that moral education and martial prowess, as tools of governance, should be balanced.

Influenced by the principles in Western Zhou Dynasty, rulers during the Spring and Autumn period were committed to prioritizing virtue in governance. People praised governance of King Wen as "great states feared his might; small states cherished his virtue" [30]. Yet as "De(virtue)" declined, an era of "eroded kingly ways and rampant hegemonism" emerged, in the context of which, Han Fei (the representative figure of legalism) pointed out that "De(virtue)" prevailed in Zhou Dynasty had been falling as the development of the society and rise of territorial wars, power and force were what the states could rely on for survival. So he held that people in ancient times were eager for virtue, people in the Middle Ages pursued wisdom, and people today strive for power [31]. Thus, the concept of "virtue" that had sustained the political order for centuries since the Western Zhou Dynasty had become obsolete amid the land consolidation and mutual encroachment among feudal lords. Han Feizi believed that in such turbulent times, "power" and "force" alone constituted the foundation for a state to survive the chaos and achieve hegemony. The Warring States period had already undermined the very foundations upon which the Western Zhou's principles of "virtue" and "ritual propriety" had been built. Falling of morality and rite led disintegration of social institutions and the evolution of virtue.

Responding to the rising hegemony and disintegrating rites, Confucianism championed the value of "De(virtue)" in governance and believed that the king should not make his people obey through force, then the concept of benevolent rule was proposed. Mencius sharply distinguished "kingly way" from "hegemonic way". A ruler following the kingly way may root his governance in "De(virtue)", rejecting coercive rule. Subduing through force is no true kingship. Mencius condemned hegemon lords as culprits against the Three Dynasties' sage-kings. In truth, the distinction between "the kingly way" and "the hegemonic way" lies not merely in whether one subjugates others through virtue or force, but in the ultimate purpose of governance. He idealized benevolent governance that fulfilled popular welfare and moral education. Mencius's starting point was the people, not the state or the sovereign. Consequently, his political ideal was benevolent governance that enabled the populace to live in peace and prosperity, rather than the pursuit of a unified empire as the ultimate political goal. For Mencius, force was not necessary for a king and unification was the outcome not purpose of benevolent governance and those who conducted force with feigning benevolence were defined hegemony. Because they just instrumentalized benevolence and virtue as legitimacy veneer.

Moreover, it serves as a crucial distinction between "the kingly way" and "the hegemonic way", and an essential criterion for judging political legitimacy. A state governed by "the kingly way" pursues benevolent governance as its political objective, cultivating moral governance internally while opposing all external military campaigns. Conversely, a state governed by "the hegemonic way" aims for grand unification as its political goal, where so-called benevolence and righteousness and moral instruction are merely means to cloak its own political legitimacy. Hence, Mencius profoundly observed: "He who employs force to feign benevolence is a Hegemon".

It was precisely based on the understanding of "De(virtue)" and "Xing(penalty)" in the Spring and Autumn period that an ideological system of attaching equal importance to virtue and punishment, or balancing leniency and severity. The principle of alternating between civil and military governance is connected to the hegemon's doctrine of balancing virtue and punishment during the Spring and Autumn period. Through Confucianism's differing value judgements on "virtue versus force" and "king versus hegemonic ruler", one can discern the choices made by Confucians during the Spring and Autumn period between these two distinct political principles. This political principle, intrinsically linked to the traditional concept of "virtue", exerted a profound influence on the selection of political thought and social governance models from the Han Dynasty onward. Confucian scholars in Han Dynasty, learning from Qin's overreliance on punishment and force and its rapid collapse, advocated the virtue of "De(virtue)" while condemning hegemonic realpolitik. Confucian's choice on "virtue and force" as well as "the kingly way and the hegemonic way" reflected its attitude toward "De(virtue)" and "Xing(penalty)".

Evolving from "balancing gentle and tough strategy" to "alternating civil or martial approaches", "De(virtue)" and "Xing(penalty)" developed into two social governance models rooted due to the debate between Confucian and Legalist, based on which, Confucians in the Han Dynasty put forward their political and legal thoughts with consideration of the landscape at that time. The concepts of "virtue" and "punishment", representing the dual political principles of conciliation and conquest since the Western Zhou Dynasty, evolved into symbols of two distinct models of social governance. This pivotal transformation commenced amid the intellectual debates between Confucian and Legalist schools during the pre-Qin period.

Bibliography

1. Wu, S. C. (2001). The origin of De (Virtue)—Legal culture in the formation of Virtue in pre-Qin period. *Chinese Journal of Law, 2.*
2. Xu, Z. S. (1998). *Dictionary of inscriptions on bones or tortoise* (p. 168). Sichuan Lexicographical Press.
3. *The Book of History · Pangeng*
4. Wang, L. (2002). *Dictionary of old Chinese by Wang Li* (p. 300). Zhonghua Book Company.
5. *The Book of History · Xi Bo Kan Li*
6. Wang, G. W. (1959). *On the system of Yin and Zhou. Guan Tang Ji Lin* (p. 451). Zhonghua Book Company.
7. *The Book of History · Cai Zhong Zhi Ming*
8. Wang, G. W. (1959). *On the system of Yin and Zhou. Guan Tang Ji Lin* (p. 451). Zhonghua Book Company.
9. Yoshihiko, O. (1983). *Virtue and hegemony in Zuo's commentary on the Spring and Autumn annals-formation and development of "virtue"* (Vol. 7, pp. 1–23). Translation of Study of Chinese History by Japanese Scholars. Zhonghua Book Company.
10. Yan, F. (1981). *Del'esprit des lois* (pp. 3 and 7). The Commercial Press.
11. Zuo's Commentary on the Spring and Autumn Annals · The 12th Year of Xuangong's Rule
12. Yoshihiko, O. (1983). *Virtue and hegemony in Zuo's commentary on the Spring and Autumn annals-formation and development of "virtue"* (Vol. 7, p. 2). Translation of Study of Chinese History by Japanese Scholars. Zhonghua Book Company.
13. Wu, S. C. (2001). The origin of Xing (Penalty)—Legal culture in the formation of penalty prior to Qin Dynasty. *Chinese Journal of Law,* 4.
14. *Yan Tie Lun·Zhao Sheng*
15. *The History of Han Dynasty·Treatise of Punishment*
16. *The Book of Zhou*: : It was your greatly distinguished father, the king Wen, who was able to illustrate his virtue and be careful in the use of punishments. He did not dare to treat with contempt (even) wifeless men and widows. He employed the employable, and revered the reverend; he was terrible to those who needed to be awed - so getting distinction among the people. It was thus he laid the foundations of (the sway of) our small portion of the kingdom, and the one or two (neighbouring) regions were brought under,

his improving influence, until throughout our western land all placed in him their reliance. This indicates care for the well-being of the people.
17. Li, G. C., & Zhang, G. H. (2001). *The history of Chinese legal thoughts* (p. 127). Shanxi People's Press.
18. Tao, X. S. (2009). *The history of Chinese political thoughts* (p. 46). Encyclopedia of China Publishing House.
19. Zuo's Commentary on the Spring and Autumn Annals · The 12th Year of Xuangong's Rule
20. Zuo's Commentary on the Spring and Autumn Annals · The 15th Year of Xigong's Rule
21. Zuo's Commentary on the Spring and Autumn Annals · The 7th Year of Wengong's Rule
22. Yoshihiko, O. (1993). *Virtue and hegemony in Zuo's commentary on the Spring and Autumn annals-formation and development of "Virtue"* (Vol. 7, p. 4). Translation of Study of Chinese History by Japanese Scholars. Zhonghua Book Company.
23. Yoshihiko, O. (1970). *Study of political thoughts in ancient China* (pp. 78–79). Qing. Aoki Shoten Publishing Co.
24. *The Book of History · Hong Fan*
25. *Records of the Grand Historian·Song Wei Zi Annoted by Zheng Xian*
26. *The Book of Change Yao*
27. *The Book of Changes·Explanation of the Trigram*
28. Zhang, T. Y. (1995). *Lecture on traditional Chinese Studies* (p. 172). East China Normal University Press.
29. *Yi Zhou Shu*
30. *Zuo's commentary on the Spring and Autumn annals—The 31st year of Xianggong's Rule*
31. *Han Fei Zi·Five Du*

CHAPTER 2

Clarification of "De(virtue)" and "Xing(penalty)" in Confucianism

1 Opposition Between "De(virtue)" and "Xing(penalty)" in Confucianism and Legalism in the Pre-Qin Period

Since the pre-Qin period, the concept of "De(virtue)" has indicated more than a ruling strategy with moral civilization as the center. During the Western Zhou Dynasty, "De(virtue)" primarily indicated the legitimacy demanded of regime, representing an ideal of benevolent governance. "Demonstration of virtue and cautious use of punishment" and "for the end of punishment is to promote virtue" were the ruling strategies taking penalty or punishment as means to achieve virtue. "Jiao(civilization)" which was involved in the concept of "De(virtue)" was another governing tool with different "appearance" to "Xing(penalty)". The saying, "when it is not necessary to put people to death (at once), let them be taught for a time", which could be summarized as "educate first, if it doesn't work, then conduct penalty", was the reflection of the relationship between "Jiao(civilization)" and "Xing(penalty)". "De(virtue)", which was the support of the people, was the foundation of governance. To win popular allegiance, moral civilization was far more effective than cruel punishments, which would lead to widespread resentment. But it didn't mean prioritizing education over punishment, nor should it be misunderstood as making education primary and punishment secondary. Precisely

D. Li, *Conceptual History of Morality and Penalty in China*, Key Concepts in Chinese Thought and Culture,
https://doi.org/10.1007/978-981-95-9059-9_2

due to the severity of punishment, people in the Zhou Dynasty paid greater attention to its consequences and discussed punishment far more frequently than education.

Inherited from the Western Zhou conception of "De(virtue)", Confucian during the Pre-Qin period further expanded it to benevolent governance, imposing virtuous demands on ruling. Here, "De(virtue)" is not merely an end but also a model representing good governance, opposing to the Legalist doctrine of "governing by law", which can be termed "rule by punishment". The opposition between "rule by punishment" and "virtue-based governance" is not, as some scholars suggest, merely a difference in strategy with the same ultimate goal. They are two different ruling models rooted in fundamentally divergent values and political philosophies. In the Han Dynasty, "De(virtue)" and "Xing(penalty)" still represented opposing governance models. However, after intellectual debates and political practices, Confucians eventually reconciled the idea of Confucianism and Legalism, choosing "De(virtue)" while also incorporating beneficial elements from the doctrine "rule by punishment" advocated by legalist in Pre-Qin period. Based on such virtue-based governance, debates on the relationship between virtue and penalty evolved.

I. Divergent Objectives of Social Governance

1. Distinctions Between Kingly Rule and Hegemonic Rule

"Kingly rule" is a central concept in Confucianism and gradually become an ideal political vision and a standard for evaluating governance after the interpretations of successive Confucian thinkers. Mencius' assertion that "conducting force with feigning benevolence defines hegemony" became a foundational criterion for Confucians in assessing the legitimacy of regimes. Kang Youwei, in *Annotations on Mencius*, argued that, even revered as Li Shimin (the second empire of the Tang Dynasty) and Zhao Kuangyin (the first empire of the Song Dynasty) could only be deemed "hegemonic" by Mencius' standards; figures like Zhu Yuanzhang (founder of the Ming Dynasty) and Ying Zheng (founder of the Qin Dynasty) were outright tyrants. "Kingly rule" serves as a moral benchmark to critique tyranny and evaluate the legitimacy of regime, furthermore, an aspirational political ideal pursued by Confucian. The concept was articulated by Mencius first, later elaborated by Xun Kuang (another representative figure of Confucianism), it became a defining political vision upheld by Confucian.

Mencius believed that human beings are born with a good nature and equal human dignity, based on which "kingly rule" could function. Furthermore, Mencius insisted that the exercise of power must align with "righteousness", advocating governance should benefit the people while opposing rulers' selfish interests. This moral distinction is essential to the legitimacy of "kingly rule". Many scholars identify "benevolent governance", which is built upon "humaneness" put forward by Confucius as the heart of Mencius' philosophy. Yet, when examining through the lens of "kingly rule", benevolent governance emerges as its intrinsic requirement. Both "benevolent governance" and "kingly rule" emphasizes meeting the people's needs, securing their livelihoods, and ensuring their well-being in life and death. As Mencius stated, this is the first step of "kingly rule".

Mencius distinguished between "kingly rule" and "hegemonic rule". He held that one who subdued others through virtue is a true king, while one who relied on force while feigning benevolence is a hegemon. The essence of "subduing men by virtue" lay not in domination but in "virtue" itself. For Mencius, the goal of governance is not external supremacy—attracting foreign states through benevolent rule—but internal well-being, ensuring the people's prosperity and stability. "De(virtue)" should be the ultimate goal for the rulers, while political influence was merely a secondary effect of achieving virtuous governance.

Does "subduing men by virtue" means opposing punishment and thus neglecting law? Mencius did indeed oppose excessive punishment and rarely discussed law, but this does not mean he was fundamentally opposed to "the rule of law". He once stated, "let them be put to death in the way which is intended to preserve their lives, and though they die, they will not murmur at those who put them to death". Punishment itself is not the goal—rather, its purpose lies in the way of preserving life, protecting the lives and well-being of the majority. Therefore, those who endanger the safety and property of people must be punished. This reveals that Mencius did not categorically reject punishment but instead emphasized its function in safeguarding the people's livelihood. He held that, punishment was not to suppress the people but to protect them, ensuring justice rather than oppression.

2. Distinctions Between Strengthening the State and Strengthening the People

Given to the profound understanding of the relationship between human nature and institutional structure in pre-Qin period, through Confucius's interpretation, Confucian humanism was deeply integrated into traditional rites, leading to a humanistic transformation of ritual. The driving force of such change was "humaneness" put forward by Confucius. Interpreting "ritual" through the lens of "humaneness" and practicing "humaneness" through "ritual", Confucius pointed, to restrain desire and practice rite, is perfect virtue.

A dialogue that Confucius traced the Zhou ritual of three-year mourning [1] to the natural affection between parent and child was recorded in *The Analects* demonstrates. By grounding the entire system of rites in filial piety, which itself stemmed from the simple love between parents and children, Confucius shifted the basis of ritual observance from external coercion—or even religious mysticism—to inner psychological sincerity. As he remarked, if you feel at ease (in shortening the mourning period), then do so. Thus, ritual became humanized by deriving its legitimacy from everyday human emotions rather than divine commandments. As Li Zehou observed, the transformation from divine decrees to human desires and conscious awareness, from submission to gods to submission to humanity—and ultimately to oneself—marked an epochal shift in the history of ancient Chinese thought [2].

The institution put forward by Confucian is grounded on the sound human nature, and all the well-intentioned laws and ideals for social governance were aimed at cultivating well-rounded moral character, fostering independent and autonomous individuals within society. Confucian holds that all human beings share undeniable common traits, based on which, everyone can, through effort, become a sage. The equality advocated by Confucian differs significantly from that of Legalist, which called for equality among people when responding to an exalted monarch—an equality where all prostrate themselves at the feet of a single ruler. In Confucianism, the nature of ordinary people and sages are the same, with no innate distinctions of worthiness, foolishness, wisdom, or incompetence. From the equality of human nature, Confucian further discusses the dignity of personhood. More importantly, it extends to the implication of universal values. If human nature is the same and human hearts are interconnected, then the values and principles of the world should be universal.

Mencius repeatedly stated in his writings that "all people can be Yao and Shun(two great kings in ancient China)", emphasizing that Yao, Shun, and ordinary people share the same human nature. As Kang Youwei pointed out, "all human nature is good; even Yao and Shun were merely embodiments of this good nature; thus, Yao and Shun are equal to everyone. This is Mencius's way of clarifying that everyone ought to be equal—a principle that reaches its zenith in the era of Great Unity and Universal Harmony. And so, people must not abandon themselves to violence or degradation, lest they forfeit their potential to become like Yao and Shun" [3]. In Mencius's view, human equality is based on the innate goodness within human nature, which is not exclusive to sages but is also possessed by the public. Therefore, equality advocated by Confucian is rooted in the idea that everyone is an independent and dignified individual.

Different from Confucian, which takes perfecting individual character as the goal of governance, Legalist explicitly advocates "weakening the people" in pursuit of state power. As *The Book of Lord Shang* declares, weakening people delivers a strong state, and a strong state means weakening people; therefore, a country that follows the right path focuses on weakening the people [4]. To "weaken the people" means to erode their autonomy and independent personhood, forcing them to rely entirely on the state for survival and advancement. In this way, the ruler's punishments and rewards would hold absolute authority, leaving the people powerless to resist.

As the people are weakened, the ruler's dominance is elevated to supremacy. In Shang Yang's view, the relationship between the state and the people was a zero-sum game. To strengthen state power, the people's autonomy and living space must be diminished. Only when the people's self-sufficiency declines would state-controlled incentives (such as ranks and rewards) become effective, thus officials gain greater authority. To weaken people, the ruler shall encourage "denunciation of criminals" and enforce "collective responsibility", for which, according to Shang Yang's system, people divided into groups of five, requires mutual surveillance, and those who reports crimes would be rewarded, while those who fails to report are punished alongside the offenders. Under such governance, the people are monitored, and their values homogenize via punishments and rewards. The ultimate goal is to mold the populace into pliable clay figures—what Shang Yang termed "controlling the people". In the framework of legalism, the state's omniscience over its subjects ensures control to penetrate every corner of society. Legalists never valued the individual; the people are merely tools for enriching and empowering the state. Even the principle about "loving the people" or "benefiting the people" is, at best, a means to cultivate obedient subjects—human livestock for the state's machinery. A state might be well-ordered under such a system, but the people could never be truly independent individuals. Far from embodying human-centered values, such governance elevated the state at the expense of the person.

II. Divergent Approaches to Social Order Formation

1. Endogenous Social Order vs. Imposed Social Order

The Confucian ideal of social order emerges through the exemplary conduct and moral guidance of the men of virtue—creating a society governed by virtue. Such order does not rely on the institutional designs of enlightened rulers but on the cultivation of rites and social customs under the leadership of the men of virtue to adjust interpersonal relationships and stabilize society. As Ruth Benedict observed, individuals in any cultural system act under the influence of social norms and customs, which implies that people can hardly escape the shaping force of their societal traditions—customs play a far greater role in molding behavior than individuals do in altering customs. Cultural patterns, including education and moral cultivation, are socially recognized behavioral standards. Rite education advocated by Confucian means to establish a cultural model that elevates individual morality while transforming societal habits to guide collective behavior. Chen Lai notes that the ritual-music civilization in Western Zhou Dynasty fostered a "methodical way of life", with derived norms meticulously regulating all aspects of communal living [5]. Inheriting this tradition, Confucians in pre-Qin period deliberately secularized religious rituals, infusing them with humanistic meaning. For instance, ancestral rites—originally purely religious—are reinterpreted as vehicles for filial piety. As the *Book of Rites* states, the repairing of the ancestral temple and the reverential performance of the sacrifices are intended to teach the people to follow their dead with their filial duty [6], linking sacrificial rituals to social ethics, aimed to highlight the cultural significance of rites as a state institution in maintaining social order.

Confucian rites encompass both the grand tradition of institutionalized rituals and the minor tradition of folk customs. The latter refers not to rigid dogma but to "moral cultivation" aimed at refining social mores. A key feature of Confucian grassroots virtue education is its non-coercive, permeating influence—shaping individual and political actions through cultural models and habits. When discussing moral education, Confucian emphasizes its cultural and social dimensions, embedding ethical and cultural rationality into ritual-music cultivation. Such humanistic approach to governance focuses on subtly shaping social order through acculturation, starkly contrasting with the Legalist model of order imposed by coercive laws.

As it noted before, "virtue" was closely tied to the ideal of kingly rule in the pre-Qin period, with "virtuous governance" manifesting as kingly rule, and moral education serving as its primary social instrument. In contrast, governance model of legalism characterized by punishment produces diametrically opposite societal effects. Where Confucian virtue education benefits generations, Legalist rule leaves behind a legacy of control, not cultivation. In contrast, the social governance model of legalism was defined by its reliance on penalty, and its societal outcomes differed markedly from the Confucian approach, which emphasized moral cultivation and left a lasting legacy for future generations.

Confucian emphasizes the significance of "rule by virtue" is shaping individuals and actively cultivating moral sentiments through the social order rooted from rite and moral education. The nurturing of individual moral character contributes to the realization of Confucian ritual-music education. By fostering personal ethical development, Confucian cultivates the gentry and virtuous individuals who serve as autonomous forces in civil society. Their exemplary conduct establishes them as moral paragons within their communities, earning them public trust and authority. Consequently, they play a pivotal role in grassroots governance.

Compared to the social order formed by Confucianism through moral influence, which subtly shapes human behavior, the social order advocated by Legalist is entirely constructed through authoritarian decrees. As the sociopolitical landscape evolves during the Spring and Autumn and Warring States periods, the traditional ethical order underpinned by clan-based politics was obsolete, leading to the collapse of associated virtue-ritual traditions. The emerging social order could no longer form spontaneously through these inherited norms; instead, it had to be forcibly established via Legalist reforms imposed by rulers. Institution supported by legalist represented a radical departure from to the traditional "virtue-based" society. The Legalist dismissed the Confucian classics (*Book of Songs*, *Book of Documents*) as antiquated and banned them, condemning the principle of familial affection as a source of selfishness and requiring people prioritize absolute public duty over private sentiments.

The state system that legalism aimed to construct was fully integrated, from values to social norms, centering solely on state-mandated laws. Government officials, as state representatives, are tasked with enforcing these laws, thereby becoming symbols of social authority. An individual's political and social standing is determined exclusively by military merit. A society that takes law as its doctrine inevitably relied on externally imposed legal standards, upending traditional ritual-music customs, and such norms could not be internalized by people following the traditional cultural mode. Therefore, the Legalist outright rejects the ways of ancient kings, aiming to construct a new social order devoid of clan-based traditions.

Taking law as doctrine means enforcing statutes as the sole benchmark for all social conduct, customs, and even moral values. The Legalist believes that a strong state is delivered through the development of agriculture and military. Thus, any tradition incompatible with Legalist doctrine—particularly those deemed irrelevant to agriculture and warfare—should be abolished. That is the reason why the legalist exhibits intense hostility toward Confucian moral and cultural traditions, labeling them "the six parasites", under which, there were twelve things. When these twelve things emerging, the ruler would be unable to make people farm and fight, and then the state would be so poor that it would be dismembered.

In summary, "rule by virtue" supported by Confucian is maintained through the subtle influence of cultural norms such as rites and moral education, shaping individual behavior. Such virtue-centered order essentially stems from the traditional cultural customs and ethical standards of the nation, forming naturally. In contrast, "rule by punishment" advocated by legalist is underpinned by the decrees of the ruler. The people adhere to this order not out of spontaneous or conscious will but are driven by the incentives of "punishments and rewards", resulting in a social order enforced by external coercion.

2. The Role of Individuals in the Formation of Social Order

The Legalist regards the people as tools for the ruler to enrich the state and strengthen its military, measuring an individual's worth solely by their utility to the ruler. Hence, the Legalist advocates the strategy of "weakening the people", aiming to diminish their capacity and will to resist the state. In contrast, Confucian views the moral cultivation of each individual as the very purpose of governance, emphasizing respect for and the development of human nature in sociopolitical life. Moreover, Confucian recognizes the critical role of morally refined individuals in shaping a well-ordered society.

Trying to figure out how to cultivate "new citizens", Liang Qichao noted the political and ethical value inherent in "rule by virtue" and sought to explore its positive elements for transforming national character and establishing modern civic order. He pointed, Confucians firmly believed that without sound citizens, there could be no sound politics; hence, its discourse on governance focused on nurturing the political morality, political capability, and political habits of the majority [7]. In his view, rites and ritual-music-based education of Confucian aimed to cultivate the people's morality and become well-rounded citizens. Once the people were morally sound, there would be no need for sage-kings or enlightened rulers to steer or lead them, nor for coercive punishments or political oppression—good governance would naturally emerge.

In the theory of Confucian, the role of the individual in shaping social order can be analysed as following.

First, the relationship between the individual and the laws regulating society. Confucian holds that institutions related to rites, music, punishments, and governance should be deeply rooted in and follow human nature, rather than to reshape it. In the Confucian view, both rites and laws should align with the inherent patterns of human development, rather than artificially elevate or alter human nature. Confucian recognizes that it is humans' nature to form groups and organizations for survival, in which however, the rights and obligations should be clarified, to resolve conflicts in interpersonal interactions. Only by organizing into societies could humans effectively conquer nature. Nevertheless, order is the key for a society to sustain, and order should entail distinctions. Xunzi acknowledged that social order is sustained by hierarchies of wealth, status, and nobility, arguing that harmony could only be achieved by embracing inequality—hence the principle of "maintaining equality through inequality". Rites, laws, and institutions are designed to sustain such hierarchical order, ensuring social harmony. Confucian does not endorse rigidly stratified hierarchies, as later critics alleged, but emphasized the spirit of "love and respect" in rites, softening the harshness of an unequal society.

Second, the relationship between the individual and the collective. "Virtue" discussed by Confucian calls for interpersonal relationships on the basis of mutual respect. Confucians regards humans as inherently communal beings—what distinguishes humans from animals is their ability to form societies. Confucius was the first to introduce the concept of "group harmony", stating that a man of virtue should be sociable but not partisan and that poetry fosters communal harmony. Xun Kuang further explained this idea, arguing that "it is humans' nature to communal life that differed them from other creatures". However, the concept of "communal life" here differs from the herd instinct of animals. Human interactions require clear boundaries of rights and duties, as well as distinctions between status and rank—what Confucians termed "human relations". Based on the understanding of human nature, Confucians posits that individual development is interdependent with collective progress. On the one hand, grounded its philosophy in the development of individuals, Confucian holds that the improvement of society and the collective relies on the moral cultivation of each person. "Man of virtue" discussed by Confucian represents the independent and dignified individual. On the other hand, it emphasizes that the development of individuals must occur as the development of others in the community. Because personal and collective advancement are mutually dependent, and the gentleman's moral development has to be guided by "righteousness", which embodies the collective interest, and "rites", which represents shared ethical norms. These principles ensures that individual aspirations harmonized with the greater good of society.

The relationship between the individual and social order in the Legalist model of "rule by punishment" stands in stark contrast to that of Confucian. Confucian respects human nature, believing in moral goodness. Thus, Confucian institutional design and social order revolve around nurturing virtuous potential in human nature. In contrast, legalism holds a skeptical view of human nature, denying any universal moral tendency toward goodness asserting that individuals are invariably motivated by self-interest. Consequently, Legalist institutions exploit such calculating nature—seeking benefit and avoiding harm—to compel the people to serve the ruler's ambitions for hegemony. The Legalists analyze human relationship through the lens of selfishness, arguing that no interpersonal bond—no matter how intimate—is purely an emotional connection. Instead, all relationships are seen as equilibriums of interest forged through exchange. Han Fei, for instance, interpreted even parent–child and ruler-subject ties as transactional arrangements stabilized by mutual calculation, stating, parents and children treat each other with a mindset of calculation [8]. Legalism examines the order of human relations from the perspective of human nature's inherent selfishness, defining all relationships as power-subordination in nature.

From this perspective, the Legalist redefines all ethical relations as hierarchies of power and subjugation, proposing the Three Bonds—the minister serves the ruler, the son serves the father, and the wife serves the husband; when these three are upheld, the world is orderly; when violated, chaos reigns [9]—this is the eternal principle of the world. Rejecting the Confucian ideal of reciprocal duties between ruler and subject, parent and child, or husband and wife, the Legalist instead enshrines the absolute authority of the ruler over the subject, the father over the son, and the husband over the wife. The Three Bonds rigidly anchor individuals within this social hierarchy, assigning each person the role of subordinate and imposing absolute obligations to obey. As a result, the governance model advocated by legalist prioritizes the state over the people and the collective over the individual, dismissing individual's role in shaping social order. The philosopher Xiong Shili critiques this approach, arguing that a healthy collective order depends on morally developed individuals. He holds that an overly rigid social organization would utterly crush individual freedom, then diminish individuals of their true nature, in the context of which, a collective wouldn't remain sound [10].

III. Different Approaches to Social Governance

Confucian prioritize moral and ritual education in social governance, stating, if the people are governed by laws and disciplined through punishments, they will avoid wrongdoing but have no sense of shame; if they are guided by virtue and harmonized through rites, they will develop a sense of shame and moreover strive to be good [11]. In the past, scholars often interpreted this as Confucius emphasizing moral education while downplaying the role of punishment in governance. Actually, Confucian virtue does not inherently exclude penalty. As previously discussed, the concept of “De(virtue)” in Western Zhou Dynasty had reflected, to some extent, feudal institution and “Sheng Fang”. In terms like “for the end of punishment is to promote virtue” and “demonstration of virtue and cautious use of punishment”, it indicates that “virtue”, as Confucian advocated, has incorporated the role of penalties, which implies penalty with prudence is an aspect of benevolent rule.

Confucian in Han Dynasty further elaborated on the concept of “moral law”. Distinguished with “heavenly law” and “penal law”不是完整句子. “Heavenly law” refers to the natural order of cosmic and seasonal cycles, reflecting the influence of the thought of Yellow Emperor and Laozi and Yin-Yang (the two opposing principles in nature). “Moral law”, synonymous with ritual norm, functions similarly to “ethical law”. Examining the relationship between virtue and punishment from a broader theoretical perspective, one may deduce the value and significance of human institutions by extrapolating from the laws and principles governing the workings of Heaven. While, “penal law” means to punish those who violated “moral law” and suppress evil, which Confucians attributed to unregulated desires. If penalties fail to curb these desires and deter wrongdoing, they would be mere tools of oppression. This discourse on “moral law” clarifies the Confucian stance on punishment under “rule by virtue”: while both “De(virtue)” and “Xing(punishment)” are employed, primacy is given to moral governance. “De(virtue)” is central to social order and serves as the ethical foundation constraining the use of punishment. From the distinction between “benevolent punishment” and “oppressive punishment” in Zhou Dynasty to debates on “penal law” versus “moral law” in Han Dynasty, Confucian had been committed to legal legitimacy rooted in moral principles.

Confucian before the Qin Dynasty held that, governance was not merely about managing the populace. Confucius framed politics as “enriching the people” and “educating the people”. True governance required not only economic prosperity but also moral cultivation to refine people’s character. From the standpoint of legitimacy, from the perspective of legitimacy, a ruler who meets the requirements of “De” must give equal weight to enriching the people and educating them. A policy that focuses solely on economic enrichment falls far short of what constitutes good governance in the Confucian sense. From the perspective of social governance measures, moral education was seen as more legitimate than harsh punishments. Ancient penal systems were notoriously brutal, with laws functioning primarily as instruments of retribution rather than normative guidance. It was recorded that five punishments encompass thousands of mutilations, from disfigurement to execution. Against this backdrop, Confucius advocated "rule by virtue", arguing that draconian laws could not inspire genuine compliance but only erode moral conscience. Lasting social order, he held, depended on moral governance that encouraged voluntary adherence to norms. As human nature was inherently inclined toward goodness, and moral education could transform hearts and minds, restoration and refining of humanity and nurture of ethical relationships, should be highlighted. As it depended on the governance of rule by virtue, imbuing daily life with ethical norms among the people would be more helpful than penalty. Punishment was not an end but a means to guide the people toward understanding the sages' teachings on human relations and natural affections. Judicial processes, when necessary, were to serve as extensions of moral edification.

Regarding the relationship between "De(virtue)" and "Xing(punishment)", Confucian emphasizes that the legitimacy of punishment lies in the ruler's prior duty to educate the people about the fundamental norms of ritual and social order, that is "teaching before punishing". As Confucius said, to punish without prior teaching is tyranny. Mencius expanded on Confucius' principle of "enrich first, then educate", arguing that the ruler should regulate the people's livelihood to ensure they have constant means of production and thus constant moral resolve. Prosperity and education are two indispensable pillars of statecraft. Without stable livelihoods and basic welfare, people, struggling for survival, will have no energy for ethical cultivation. Conversely, wealth without moral instruction leads to lawlessness, what Mencius condemned as "luring the people into crime".

The highest form of moral governance lies in subtly educating the populace through moral instruction, thereby perfecting individual character. Ultimately, societal governance is achieved through the self-disciplined of the people. "Governance by virtue" would be achieved through moral education, in the process of which, the ruler should diminish their role to minimal intervention to realize the ideal of "governing without exertion". The fundamental principle of minimizing state intervention in civil society lies in cultivating the moral character of every member through ethical education, thereby fostering the populace's capacity for self-governance. It is the highest ideal of "rule by virtue". As Mou Zongsan interpreted, "such morally transformative governance, is totally grounded in the concrete moral personality of each individual" [12].

"Virtue" invoked by Legalist diverged radically from that of Confucian. Under the model of "rule by punishment", "virtue" and "penalty" are merely way of control. For Han Fei, "virtue" means nothing more than "rewards" or "benefits"—bestowals by the ruler to incentivize officials and people. "Virtue" supported by Confucian, however, indicates both ethical cultivation and political-legal legitimacy, fostering shared values and organic social order through popular self-discipline. Though both schools acknowledged the role of virtue in governance, their interpretations differed fundamentally. While Confucian sought harmony through moral uplift and voluntary adherence, Legalist reduced "virtue" to a transactional mechanism reinforcing autocratic power.

2 Intellectual Transformation and Institutional Reform During the Qin and Han Dynasties

I. Governance Under the Influence of Thought on Yin-Yang and Five Elements

The concepts of *Yin-Yang* and the *Five Elements* were core ideas in the culture of ancient China. They originated from philosophy of *Yin-Yang* in the pre-Qin period, and were later absorbed into Confucianism and other schools of thought. They became fundamental essences in traditional Chinese philosophy and legal theory.

As Liang Qichao observed, the original meaning of *Yin-Yang* was merely a rudimentary description of natural phenomena, devoid of profound significance [13]. However, over time, these simple notions evolved beyond basic observations like *"sun-facing is Yang, shade-facing is Yin"* and were used to explain social phenomena. For instance, the *Guo Yu* recorded how the Grand Historian Bo Yangfu once used Yin-Yang to explain an earthquake that occurred during the reign of King You of Zhou Dynasty. He linked the disorder of *Yin-Yang* to political decline, arguing that the earthquake resulted from the decay of virtue, which would further lead to civil unrest, economic collapse, even the state's demise

[14]. This illustrated how *Yin-Yang* theory had transcended from natural observation to a framework for explaining political and legal order. By the Warring States period, thinkers like Zou Yan further developed the theory of *Yin-Yang*, elevating it into a dominant discourse for interpreting state affairs and legal policies.

"Five Virtues' Rotation" or "Five Virtues' Cycle" put forward by scholars developing the theory of Yin-Yang is based on the principle of "mutual conquest among the Five Elements", which follows the rule of earth overcoming water, water overcoming fire, fire overcoming metal, and wood overcoming earth. Scholars of *Yin-Yang* explain dynastic transitions and sociopolitical changes with such principle. For example, the Yellow Emperor, associated with the color yellow, corresponds to the earth element; Yu the Great, linked to green, represents wood; King Tang of Shang and King Wen of Zhou are aligned with metal and fire, respectively. Thus, Yu replacing the Yellow Emperor, Tang replacing Yu, and Wen replacing Tang—are seen as a manifestation of the Five Elements' cyclical conquest. Legitimacy of regime, in such view, depends on whether the ruler' "virtue" matches the cosmic Qi and heavenly portents. If a rising power's elemental virtue surpasses that of the incumbent regime, it signals a transfer of "Mandate of Heaven", justifying the new dynasty's rise.

The "Five Virtues' Cycle" theory are used to warn rulers to be respectful to the "Mandate of Heaven" with elemental symbolism, illustrating that regime change is ultimately a matter of cosmic destiny. This mirrors the concept of "Heaven-human resonance" advocated by Dong Zhongshu, who employed the concept of natural disasters serving as celestial warnings to urge rulers to pursue virtuous governance.

Connecting the ruler's virtue to governance models, scholars of the thought Ying-Yang asserts that "each virtue in rotation demands its appropriate governance". Virtue and punishment had been incorporated into *Yin-Yang* cosmology in the Eastern Zhou period. Virtue, representing benevolent rule, was associated with *Yang*. While punishment, symbolizing punitive force, was linked to *Yin*. Texts like the *Huangdi Sijing* written in mid-Warring States period articulated this "Yang-virtue, Yin-punishment" concept, framing the alternation of virtue and punishment as mirroring the cyclical rhythms of nature [15]. Similarly, *Guanzi* likened the application of virtue and penalty to the four seasons, advocating a balanced use of them in statecraft [16].

Though seemingly esoteric, such correlation between governance methods (*virtue/punishment*) and natural laws (*Yin-Yang/seasons*) profoundly influenced the legal and administrative construction in the Qin and Han Dynasties. According to historical records, Ying Zheng, after the unification and the foundation of Qin Dynasty, deeply believed in the doctrine of "*Five Virtues' Cycle*" advocated by the scholars developing the theory of Yin-Yang [17]. The theory's *"conquest logic"* particularly legitimized Qin's rise—a northwestern state violently supplanting the Central Plains' Six Kingdoms and the Zhou Dynasty. Some scholars argued that *the Five Virtues' Cycle doctrine played a decisive role in Qin's adoption of "rule by punishment" advocated by the Legalist* [18]. While Qin's embrace of Legalism may not have solely relied on Zou Yan's *"mystical theories"*, the *Five Virtues'* explanation for Qin's legitimacy made it one of the most impactful doctrines shaping the dynasty's legal trajectory.

According to the *Records of History*, Ying Zheng fervently believed in the theory of the "Five Virtues' Cycle". The primary reason why he continued to adhere to the Legalist "rule by punishment" as the foundation of state governance after the unification is that he held the Zhou Dynasty embodied the virtue of Fire, and since Qin succeeded Zhou, it must adopt the virtue of Water [19]. The Commentary on *the Book of Rites: The Book of Fengchan* states: Water is associated with the Yin principle, and Yin governs punishment and execution, hence, rule by punishment, which advocated by the Legalist was prioritized in the Qin Dynasty. Although the Qin's reliance on "rule by punishment" ultimately led to its collapse, the theories of *Yin-Yang* and the Five Elements were not abandoned in the Han Dynasty but were further refined. Dong Zhongshu, synthesizing these concepts with his doctrine of "Heaven-human resonance", advanced the principle of "Yang-virtue and Yin-punishment" and conducted reforms to rectify the political malpractices stemming from the Qin institutions and inherited by Han, advocating "morality-ruling over penalty-ruling". The interplay between shifts in governance models during the Qin and Han Dynasties and the underlying "Five Virtues' Cycle" theory revealed that Yin-Yang cosmology served as a critical lens for understanding the relationship between virtue and punishment from the pre-Qin era to the Han Dynasty.

II. The Malpractice of Institutions of Han Inherited from Qin Dynasty and the Significance of "Morality-Ruling over Penalty-Ruling"

1. The Malpractice of Institutions of Han Inherited from Qin Dynasty

A radical transformation in institutions and ideologies was observed during the transition from the Qin to the Han Dynasty. Unifying the states through "rule by punishment" advocated by Legalist, abolishing the enfeoffment in favor of the system of prefectures and counties, and constructing a state centered on harsh laws and severe penalties, Qin's oppressive governance ultimately sparked widespread popular resentment, leading to the dynasty's collapse after just two generations. While in the early period of Han Dynasty, influenced by the thought of the Yellow Emperor and Laozi, "rule through non-action" was prioritized, to allow the war-weary populace to recover. However, such governance failed to address the legacy of Qin's legal system. As historical records noted, the institutions and laws in early Han wholly inherited that of the Qin Dynasty. The Legalist thought of Shen Buhai and Han Fei, dominant in the late Warring States, succeeded the thought of the Emperor Huang and Laozi as the guiding principle of the Han Dynasty. This trend intensified during the reigns of Emperors Wen and Jing, marked by the suppression of the Seven Kingdoms' Rebellion, while the rise of "cruel officials" [20].

In conclusion, the governance in early Han Dynasty demonstrated two key characteristics. On the one hand, the legal system was influenced by Legalism. The Han's foundational legal code, compiled by Xiao He, largely replicated statutes in Qin Dynasty. On the other hand, the Officialdom was affected by the doctrine "rule by law". Officials like Xiao He and Cao Shen rose from criminal judges, as well as the notorious "cruel official" Zhang Tang ascended through mastery of penal law. In the early days of King Wu's ruling, more officials got promoted in this way. Their way of governance exacerbated the inherited Qin-era malpractices.

2. "Morality-Ruling over Penalty-Ruling" as a Reformation of Early Han Governance

In response to the malpractice stemming from Qin and inherited by Han Dynasty, Dong Zhongshu proposed to conduct "reformation", which aimed to overhaul the Qin's punitive governance system and its underlying ethos, serving as a corrective to historical deviations. Dong Zhongshu argued that the Legalist "rule by punishment" in Qin Dynasty had utterly destroyed the folk customs and moral traditions nurtured by rites and music in the Zhou Dynasty. Although replaced the Qin's regime, the rulers in the Han Dynasty failed to critically reflect the governance model. Though people were provided respite in the early period of Han Dynasty, the rulers did not fundamentally reform the Qin's punitive legal system or its governing philosophy. Dong Zhongshu employed a vivid metaphor in his *Three Strategies on Heaven and Humanity*, comparing such governance to "rotten wood and a dung-plastered wall", which required complete reconstruction to restore order [21].

The "reformation" he proposed here was not innovation but restoration, reviving the Confucian tradition of "rule by virtue". As Dong stated, "the great principle of the Way is decided by the Heaven; if Heaven does not change, neither does the Way". The "Way" here, guided a return to pre-Qin Confucian governance. Dong criticized early Han rulers for perpetuating the Qin's oppressive bureaucracy without reflection [21]. Therefore, the "reformation" he proposed was not merely about replacing penalties with moral education but a comprehensive substitution of Qin's "rule by punishment" with Confucian "rule by virtue". His proposals, outlined in the Three Strategies, can be summarized as "morality-ruling over penalty-ruling", with three key aspects:

First, grounding the relationship between virtue and punishment in his "heaven-human resonance" theory, Dong Zhongshu put forward morality-ruling over penalty-ruling. He asserted that "Mandate of Heaven" and "Yin-Yang calamities" were not abstract concepts but Heaven's responses to earthly governance. To retain the Mandate, rulers must practice "kingly governance", the Confucian ideal of virtuous rule. The so-called foundation of the Way of the King lies in righteousness. For a sovereign to establish the legitimacy of his rule, he must "establish the foundation of the Way of the King in righteousness". According to Dong Zhongshu's requirement, this entails governing in accordance with the Way of Heaven, ensuring that his rule does not contravene Heaven. Since Heaven operated through Yin-Yang, with virtue as Yang and punishment as Yin, and since Yang (associated with growth and nurturing) dominated Yin, governance must prioritize moral education over punitive measures.

Second, the doctrine of "rule by moral education" targeted not the people but the ruler. Dong Zhongshu argued that the people's morality directly reflected the ruler's virtue. Under the governance of Yao and Shun, the people were benevolent and harmonious, enjoying long lives;

while, under the rule of Jie and Zhou, people became corrupt and violent, leading to short lifespans. Thus, the key to moral education was not "teaching the people" but "rectifying the ruler". Only by correcting the ruler, the court, and the officials could the people be guided toward virtue. Drawing on Confucian "humaneness", Dong Zhongshu emphasized human dignity and ethical uniqueness. Humans "transcend all other beings" because they understand morality and kinship. This innate capacity for virtue meant that governance must nurture, not coerce, human nature. Ruling through rewards and punishments would violate this principle. Moral education, therefore, had to be gradual and aligned with human nature—any forced or hasty indoctrination would mutilate humanity.

Third, Dong Zhongshu's proposition of "morality-ruling over penalty-ruling" advocated, at the level of social governance, the implementation of Confucian "rule by virtue" rather than Legalist "rule by punishment". It doesn't ignore the role of punishment in governance. As the four seasons are irreplaceable in a year, both rewards and punishments in Dong's mind, were indispensable in governance [22].

Dong Zhongshu was not in an attempt to discuss "moral education" or "penalty", which one is more important, but to resist Qin's Legalist legacy, and recenter Han governance on Confucian ethics and Heaven's moral cosmology. To achieve which, first of all, the ruler should be committed to doctrine and principle with political legitimacy; the people should embrace the virtue in governance and be taught with morality as sensitive and benevolent subjects, with patience and human nature fulfillment. Teaching should not be rushed or distort human nature; it should nurture and fulfill it.

3. "Rectifying Oneself" Versus "Governing Others"

The doctrine of "morality-ruling over penalty-ruling" proposed by Dong Zhongshu strived to eradicate the Legalist "rule by punishment" inherited from the Qin and restore the Confucian tradition of "rule by virtue", which encompassed two critical dimensions: rectifying the ruler—imposing legitimacy demands on those in power; implementing moral education—cultivating the people's virtue to achieve organic social order. In the context of Han Dynasty, the core of "rule by virtue" evolved to "rectifying oneself" and "governing others", emphasizing both "first correct oneself, then correct others" [23] and "hold oneself to strict standards while being lenient toward others" [24].

Building upon Mencius' framework of "humaneness as the heart, righteousness as the path", Dong Zhongshu developed the Standards of Benevolence and Righteousness, clarifying the relationship between "humaneness" and "righteousness". Humaneness is to govern others, serving as the ethical standard for ruling the people; while righteousness is to discipline oneself, serving as the political-moral requirement for rulers [25]. Rulers must take righteousness to constrain their own conduct but employ humaneness to govern the people. That is, rulers cannot use law to forcibly implement "righteousness", meaning that law cannot forcibly promote moral progress. Dong Zhongshu's discussion of the relationship between "benevolence" and "righteousness" in terms of "governing others" and "rectifying oneself" is similar to Fuller's distinction between "aspirational morality" and "duty-based morality". What Fuller refers to as "duty-based morality" is "starting from the lowest point, it establishes the basic principles that make an ordered society possible or enable an ordered society to achieve its specific goals" [25], which is the minimum moral requirement for people.

Such distinction parallels Lon L. Fuller's classification of "aspirational morality" and "duty-based morality". As Fuller noted, duty-based morality is the basic rules without which an ordered society is impossible [26]—the minimal moral baseline enforceable by law; while aspirational morality is of the Good Life, of excellence, and of human flourishing—ethical ideals beyond legal coercion. Distinctions of the two delineate law's proper scope in advancing morality. Law could codify only the morality of duty to maintain societal order. While the aspirational morality is in the sphere of private ethical, the government shall not legislate to interfere with individuals' private moral space in the name of promoting morality.

Dong Zhongshu's differentiation between "rectifying oneself" and "governing others" serves to standardize Confucian virtue-based governance theory, preventing rulers from exploiting "righteousness" as a pretext to arbitrarily extend imperial authority into the ethical and moral domains which needs to be adjusted by the society. Dong further articulated the Confucian principles of moral education: inward governance requires introspection according to principle to rectify oneself, relying on rites to cultivate; outward governance extends kindness broadly, employing lenient systems to accommodate the multitude.

This formulation establishes two fundamental dimensions for Confucian moral education: self-rectification, which indicates the ruler must hold himself to higher ethical standards with "righteousness" and governing others, which implies the state should employ leniency to accommodate the multitude, avoiding the imposition of elite moral teachings on commoners through coercive political means.

As the above demonstrates, Dong Zhongshu posited a sequential relationship between "rectifying oneself" and "governing others". He argued that social harmony depended on the ruler's ability to practice governance and fulfill the people's nature, achievable only through Confucian moral education. Such education, however, presupposed the ruler's willingness to "discipline himself with righteousness". Only after achieving self-rectification could the ruler "transform the people through virtue".

4. Adjudicating Cases According to *Spring and Autumn Annals*: Application of "Morality-Ruling over Penalty-Ruling" in the Judicial Realm

Han inherited the institutions of the Qin Dynasty, and thus exhibited strong characteristics of legalism. The *Records of the Grand Historian* notes that the ceremonial protocols devised by Shusun Tong were essentially a hybrid of Qin's rituals and ancient Confucian rites. Moreover, emperors in the early Han Dynasty favored harsh officials to oversee punishments, which resulted in excessively severe judicial practices. Though Liu Che (Emperor Wu in Han Dynasty) promoted Confucianism under the banner of "restoring and reforming governance", his reign prioritized military expansion over cultural governance. So, Confucianism's influence on institutions remained limited for decades, functioning more as a nominal policy than a transformative force. Scholars observed that "adjudicating cases by *the Spring and Autumn Annals*"—a practice that initiated the "Confucianization of law"—represented one phase of the "Confucianization of governance". Those who adjudicated cases by *the Spring and Autumn Annals* applied benevolent forbearance of Confucian classics to legal judgments [27]. The legal system is not merely a technical amalgamation of norms but is rooted in a coherent ethical foundation and value system, intertwined with the society's political structure, moral customs, and traditions, which cannot be overhauled overnight. The norms and principles of codified law often emerge gradually from recurring cases. Adjudicating cases by the *Spring and Autumn Annals* exemplified "Confucianization of law" in practice.

The Core Principle of "adjudicating cases by *the Spring and Autumn Annals*" is "judging by intent" which is conceived to rectify the flaws of Qin's governance. In a memorial to Emperor Wu, Dong Zhongshu criticized law of Qin Dynasty for its rigid formalism that clashed with human sentiment—a contradiction between external norms and internal will. Confucian has always strived the harmony between outward rules and inward reasons. However, the legal system in Qin and Han Dynasties, rooted in the Legalist principle of "holding actualities to its name", degenerated into an excessive focus on behavioral compliance while ignoring subjective motives and feelings. Reality presents endlessly varied cases with complex psychological underpinnings. To regulate such human complexity with simplistic, inflexible laws would "cut feet to fit shoes". Moreover, "law" in ancient China essentially meant "punishment". An exclusive emphasis on external compliance inevitably led to draconian penalties. Dong Zhongshu argued that proper justice must investigate both factual contexts and inner states, asserting:

"In *Spring and Autumn* adjudication, verdicts must be grounded in facts while probing intent. Those with wicked motives are punished preemptively; ringleaders face harsher penalties; the well-intentioned receive leniency" [28].

Thus, identical acts could yield different judgments based on the perpetrator's intent, that is deciding cases by examining hearts; those who err against the law with good intent are exempt; those who comply with the law with evil intent are condemned [29]. This approach sought to mitigate legal rigidity by harmonizing human sentiment with jurisprudence. The *Spring and Autumn Adjudications* records a dispute:

A had a son B, given to C for adoption in infancy and raised by C. As an adult, B struck A with a stick after A drunkenly revealed, "you are my son". A sued B for "a son striking his father".

Dong Zhongshu held, though A was B's biological father, he had severed paternal bonds by relinquishing upbringing to C. Thus, B's act shouldn't be punished as "assaulting one's father" [30].

Without citing from *Spring and Autumn* or other precedents directly, Dong abstracted Confucian ethics into a judicial principle, correcting the injustice in mechanical legal application. Since Confucius, Confucian prioritized substance over form, valuing emotional truth over superficial compliance. All norms—whether laws, rites, or music—were but appearance to innate human feelings, existing to accommodate and regulate these sentiments. Under such philosophy, Confucian adjudication should align with human reason and moral principle.

Strict textual adherence and achieving of justice had always been a fundamental tension in legal history. Strict application may prevent judicial abuse and enforce deterrence, but risks mechanistic outcomes. Flexible interpretation prioritizes justice, yet may undermine consistency. In ancient China, where law equated to penal sanctions, legalist-style formalism inevitably bred excessive harshness. While rigid codification could curb official corruption in authoritarian regimes, its collateral injustices were often irreparable. Confucianism's insistence on contextualized, ethically informed adjudication thus humanized judicial abuse, tempering its severity and makes the practice of traditional law more humane.

Adjudicating by *the Spring and Autumn*, knocked the door of taking Confucian canonical principles as the judicial basis, under which, the thought of benevolent governance and penalty with prudence played a profound role in the governance and legal practice in the early period of Han Dynasty and largely dwarfed the influence of "severe punishment" in legal system. This effectively eased the contradiction and stabilized the society.

III. The Practice of Moral Civilization by "Xun Li" in the Han Dynasty

Due to the efforts of Confucian scholars like Dong Zhongshu, the political ideal of "rule by virtue and rites" gradually took root—not only accepted by rulers but also implemented by grassroots officials embodying Confucian principles. These officials, known as "Xun Li" (law-abiding officials with human affection), were either "strict conformists to laws and rules" or "vigorous practitioners of moral education".

The term "Xun Li" first appeared in the *Records of the Grand Historian*, where Sima Qian dedicated a biography section to officials who "followed laws and principles without boasting of achievements or abilities, leaving no notable praise or blame among the people" [31]. Ban Gu, another historian deeply influenced by Confucianism, also compiled a *Biographies of Virtuous Officials*, though his criteria differed slightly. For Ban Gu, "Xun Li" were those who excelled in implementing Confucian "rule by virtue" in local governance. Wen Weng, governor of Shu commandery, who was renowned for "benevolence and dedication to education" and Huang Ba, a "lenient" administrator, who "prioritized moral transformation before punishment" were characterized by "self-discipline, reverence to predecessors, incorruptibility, and avoidance of harshness", achieving popular civilization. While, officials who "excelled in their posts but relied heavily on penalties" earned Ban Gu's respect but not the title of "Xun Li".

As we mentioned before, Dong's doctrine of "morality-ruling over penalty-ruling" emphasizes both "governing the people" and "rectifying oneself", which indicates that rulers and scholars must "introspect according to principle to correct themselves". The "principle" here aligns with Sima Qian's "conforming to laws and principles". From the words and actions in The Biographies of Exemplary Officials, Sima Qian's so-called upholding laws and following principles actually places more emphasis on "following principles". Statutes contrary to "principle" should be disregarded, while just laws should be enforced in ways acceptable to the people. Specifically, the "principle" followed by the administrative officials mainly reflected Dong Zhongshu's requirement for scholars and gentlemen to "return to principles and rectify themselves". A prime example is Gongyi Xiu, a "Xun Li" who followed laws without alteration, making officials self-corrected. He forbade his family from weaving for sale growing vegetables, declaring, those who receive official salaries must not compete with commoners for profit; those granted great privileges must not seek minor gains, which echoes what recorded in *Three Strategies on Heaven and Humanity*: high-ranking officials should not pursue petty profits or vie with the people for livelihoods[32]. Thus, "Xun Li" advocated by Sima Qian epitomizes Dong's ideal of "introspect according to principle to correct themselves" [33]. Overall, we believe that the "law-abiding officials" recorded in the Records of the Grand Historian more reflect Dong Zhongshu's moral governance thought on the requirement of "self-correction", serving as the best example of Dong Zhongshu's idea of "rectifying oneself by adhering to principles".

Expanding on Dong's notion of "extending kindness broadly", "Xun Li" advocated by Ban Gu is the one seeking equilibrium between legal rigor and human empathy. As Ban Gu noted, "Xun" means to comply with public laws and human feelings. It is possible to explore the practice of "rule by virtue" of Han Dynasty model officials by examining the words and actions of the officials recorded in "Biography of Model Officials".

1. Promoting Education to Cultivate Public Virtue

The *Biographies of Virtuous Officials* recorded how Wen Weng, Governor of Shu, observed the region he governed was in a remote location and lack of cultured customs. In response, he established schools to nurture men of virtue who would serve as moral exemplars in rural society. They not only set ethical standards but also took on quasi-official roles in grassroots governance—organizing agricultural production and mediating disputes. Besides, Huang Ba, who was also the model "Xun Li" praised in *The History of the Han Dynasty* governed Yingchuan through appointing officials to propagate imperial decrees, ensuring public understanding of state policies and selecting respected elders as neighborhood leaders to encourage virtue and monitor misconduct. Through such local exemplars, Huang achieved moral civilization to the people while promoted agriculture to enrich the people.

2. Advancing Public Welfare to Secure Livelihoods

"Xun Li" was not merely a moralist but a practitioner who actively improved economic conditions. Zhao Xinchen, Governor of Nanyang, was renowned for devotion to public welfare, prioritizing prosperity [34]. Huang Ba, who combined moral instruction with poverty alleviation, removed exploitative practices. What Sima Qian and Dong Zhongshu emphasized revealed the connotation of Confucianism from different aspects. "Xun Li" described by Sima Qian focused on "adhering to principle", embodying the ideal of "self-rectification", strictly observing the Confucian tenet that "officials must not compete with the people for profit". While "Xun Li" described by Ban Gu practiced the Confucian maxim "first enrich, then educate" and personally engaged in farming to inspire productivity, believing economic stability underpinned moral transformation (as wind bends grass, so do gentlemen influence the people).

Through an examination of "Xun Li" in the Han Dynasty, we find that "morality-ruling over penalty-ruling" indicates neither mere a strategy to substitute penalty by virtue, nor rule by man. It is a thorough rectification of "rule by penalty" in the Qin Dynasty, representing a tremendous shift on social governance.

Rule by virtue" advocated by Confucian fundamentally emphasizes the legitimacy of governance, requiring that rulers, their policies, and institutional designs align with virtue, which represents a significant advancement over Legalism that prioritizes rule by authority and rule by punishment without any notion of legitimacy. For Legalists, expanding the ruler's territory and wealth is the ultimate goal of a regime. "Xun Li" under the influence of Confucian conducts virtuous governance by first constraining their own conduct through moral discipline. "Xun Li" who is praised by Sima Qian as "strictly conformed to laws and rules", introspect according to principle to correct themselves. For example, Gongyi Xiu, who upheld the principle that "those granted great privileges must not seek minor gains", rejected official profiteering at the people's expense. Li Li, a judicial officer, who committed suicide after mistakenly sentencing an innocent man to death. Though his superior blamed Li's subordinates, Li insisted on accepting responsibility as the supervising official, declaring that leaders must answer for their actions—even without censure [32]. This reflected the Confucian ideal of the minister as a moral agent: one who serves the ruler with principle and propriety, retains independent judgment that follows the Way, not the ruler, and upholds personal integrity when ethical governance is thwarted. This, although applicable to handling the relationship between ruler and subject, can also derive the independent value judgment of Confucian officials to "follow the Way rather than the ruler

Legalists viewed ruler-subject and ruler-populace relations as inherently adversarial—a temporary alliance forged through self-interest. In contrast, Confucian moral education aimed not merely to elevate public virtue but to reconcile state-society tensions. By replacing harsh laws with shared values, it mitigated resentment from draconian punishments and fostered a common ethical framework enabling self-governance. "Xun Li" and scholar-officials, serving as the cultural intermediary, softly transmitted imperial decrees while grounded state authority in grassroots moral norms. Combining rank-bestowal ceremonies with communal feasts emerged in the Han Dynasty, Japanese scholars fused autocratic power with the moral appeal of the rank system [35]. For instance, Governor Huang Ba of Yingchuan bridged the gap between inaccessible imperial edicts and local communities by appointing village elders to teach Confucian values and selecting upright clerks to explain decrees in vernacular terms. By shaping people's mind through education, the state power permeated society through cultural persuasion rather than coercion. Modern scholars argue this demonstrates how the integration of moral education with imperial authority allowed Confucian to shape order at the lowest tiers of governance—the prefecture and county societies [36].

"Rule by punishment"—a prototype of heteronomy—treated the people as passive subjects to be controlled by penal codes. Its modern counterpart, rule of law rooted in civil society, operates on diametrically opposed principles. Confucian "rule by virtue", however, relied on local gentry imbued with Confucian values, acting as model exemplary, and leading communities in self-organizing governance mechanisms.

3 The Evolution of Confucian Thought on the Relationship Between Virtue and Punishment During the Era of a Unified Empire

During the era of a unified empire, the concept of "rule of virtue" largely carried forward the Confucian ideals from the pre-Qin period, and as always, reflected the Confucian pursuit of political legitimacy and value judgments. The requirements for political legitimacy primarily include two aspects:

First, ruling power itself should possess virtue. Successive generations of scholars inherited the pre-Qin debates between Confucian and Legalist on the "Way of Kings" and the "Way of Hegemony". They regarded rulers who practiced benevolent governance and achieved "protecting the people" as following the Way of Kings, while those who exploited the people to enrich themselves were labeled as "hegemonic". Some bold thinkers even denounced such rulers as "enemies of the people". For instance, the Song Dynasty Neo-Confucian scholar Lu Jiuyuan argued that benevolent governance lies in nurturing the people: "If a ruler fails to practice benevolent governance but instead enriches himself by extorting the people, he is aiding tyranny against people" [37]. The Ming Dynasty Confucian Fang Xiaoru further asserted that the purpose of Heaven in establishing rulers was to "nourish the people", not to "enrich and empower a single individual". Human societies require rulers for effective governance, without a strong leader to administer laws and enforce penalties, social stability cannot be achieved. Thus, the ruler's duty is to maintain order and harmony [38]. If a ruler fails in this duty, Fang Xiaoru deemed him "unfit to rule". From the principle that "Heaven establishes rulers for the sake of the people", Fang Xiaoru developed a framework for judging the legitimacy of historical regimes. He criticized Zhu Xi for indiscriminately labeling all dynasties that ruled the Central Plains as "legitimacy", arguing that this ignored the connection between political legitimacy and legitimacy. Fang Xiaoru contended that a dynasty's claim to legitimacy depended not on whether the ruler "possessed the realm", but on whether he practiced benevolent governance and ruled with virtue [39]. Whether in distinguishing between the Way of Kings and the Way of Hegemony, or debating political legitimacy versus political illegitimacy, ancient scholars operated within the pre-Qin Confucian framework of virtuous governance, demanding that politics be rooted in moral integrity.

Second, the methods of governance should embody virtue. Ancient Confucians unanimously held that virtuous governance must be rooted in benevolence. Thus, practicing benevolent governance and implementing the rule of virtue became intrinsic to the moral of governance. Earlier scholars often underestimated the significance of benevolent governance, assuming it merely meant extending kindness to the people and ruling through conciliation. Its purpose was limited to maintaining the ruler's authority, and its method relied solely on rectifying what is wrong in the sovereign's mind. Yet, in the face of autocratic monarchs, unarmed Confucian scholars' empty talks about rectifying the ruler's errors were little more than casting pearls before swine. Moreover, while political climate profoundly influences social customs, the transformation of folkways cannot be achieved overnight simply by a shift in governance.

Admittedly, "rectifying the errors in ruler's mind" could not effectively restrain imperial power—control over authority depends on institutional checks and balances and democratic institutional oversight. Under autocracy, Confucian benevolent governance or rule of virtue struggled to produce practical effects. However, it is crucial to note that Confucian benevolent governance or virtuous rule was a normative demand regarding the legitimacy of monarchical power. At its core, it sought to regulate rulers' power, and in this regard, its normative purpose does not conflict with the spirit of modern democratic constitutionalism. Confucians, operating within an agrarian economy and an autocratic social system, could not possibly have conceived modern constitutional frameworks. Therefore, criticizing them from the perspective of modern constitutionalism for failing to propose institutional mechanisms to effectively limit imperial power is both an unfair imposition on the past and an evasion of contemporary responsibility. Each generation has its historical mission: democracy and constitutionalism are inescapable duties of our generation. How can we shift this burden onto the ancients? The fact that Mencius could boldly declare before greedy, despotic rulers that enemies of the people may be slain and tyrants may be overthrown should put every modern intellectual to shame. Far from conflicting with democratic constitutionalism, Confucian benevolent governance or virtuous rule can serve as a complement to and development of modern rule of law, offering a traditional Chinese perspective on contemporary legal frameworks.

Moreover, Confucianism did not rely solely on "rectifying the ruler's mind" to achieve the transformation of social customs. Through benevolent governance and rule of virtue, Confucianism employed the gentle approach of "transformation through virtue" to gradually cultivate social customs, fostering self-governance among the people and the organic development of communal order. Compared to the Legalist "rule of punishment", the "rule of virtue" relied on scholar-gentlemen who served as a bridge within civil society. They strengthened cohesion and solidarity in grassroots rural communities, while also acting as tangible moral exemplars for the common people in their daily lives. Such genuine moral exemplars from daily life are fundamentally incomparable to the state-manufactured "model citizens" created by totalitarian propaganda machines. The latter are artificially constructed figures whose narratives often defy common sense and human authenticity, filled with hypocritical didacticism. Far from achieving virtue education, they breed pretentiousness and duplicity in society. The former, by contrast, were tangible figures in everyday life. Through their words and deeds, they subtly cultivated virtuous customs while also serving as mediators in local disputes, becoming pivotal forces for conflict resolution in rural society. Thus, that Ye Shi's criticism of the Confucian notion that "Once rectify the ruler, and the kingdom will be firmly settled". overlooked the substantial grassroots efforts of Confucian virtue governance in local communities.

From another perspective, Confucianism's efforts to refine social customs and rectify human character through virtue transformation actually enhanced the self-governing capacity of civil society. If Legalist "rule of law" primarily relied on external statutes to regulate behavior—a form of "heteronomous governance"—then Confucian "rule of virtue" required self-governance among the people. In the short term, the

Confucian approach of moral transformation, which promoted self-governance, effectively mitigated tensions between the ruler and the people, and between officials and commoners. Unlike the Legalist model, which portrayed ruler-subject relations as transient alliances of mutual exploitation, Confucian governance fostered relative harmony. In the long term, Confucian "rule of virtue" depended on local gentry imbued with Confucian values to serve as exemplars, unifying communal beliefs and consensus. They led villages in developing self-governing structures and mechanisms. These measures nurtured the organic growth of civil autonomy—much like how modern rule of law presupposes a robust civil society. Confucian virtue cultivation refined customs and aligned hearts-and-minds, fostering shared faith and value systems. Thus, Confucian virtue transformation also cultivated the latent potential for societal self-governance.

In summary, the relationship between virtue and punishment in imperial China was grounded in Confucian "rule of virtue" while incorporating pragmatic elements from Legalist "rule of punishment". Although one might describe this as "the integrated application of rites, music, and penal law", "virtue", and "punishment" were not merely a matter of primary versus secondary emphasis. They differed not only in status but also in their fundamental nature and function. During the unified empire, "punishment" had been reduced to an instrumental means, while "virtue" was not merely a means but rather the foundational mode of social governance. Functionally, "virtue" constituted the root of governance, defining the basic model and underlying spirit of ancient Chinese social governance, whereas "punishment" served as its practical application—a supplementary means employed in the implementation of "rule of virtue". Thus, in brief, the virtue-punishment dynamic of the unified empire can be characterized as "virtue as the foundation with punishment as the instrument". Only by recognizing "virtue" as the root can one truly grasp the distinctive features of ancient governance models. As the eminent legal historian Chen Guyuan observed: "In the formation of the Chinese legal tradition, if we consider the establishment of its systematic framework, it becomes clear that while the Legalists constructed its skeletal structure, it was the Confucians who endowed it with its soul" [40].

Bibliography

1. *Analects·Yang Huo.*
2. Li, Z. H. (2008). *History of thought in ancient China (New Version)* (p. 21). TASS Publishing House.
3. Kang, Y. W. (1987). *Meng Zi Wei* (p. 15). Zhonghua Book Company.
4. *The book of Lord Shang·weaken the people.*
5. Chen, L. (1996). *Ancient religion and ethics* (p. 9). SDX Joint Publishing Company.
6. *The book of rite·Fang Ji.*
7. Liang, Q. C. (2004). *History of political thought pirior to Qin dynasty* (p. 98). Tianjin Classic Press.
8. *Han Fei Zi · Six Fan.*
9. *Han Fei Zi · Zhong Xiao.*
10. Xiong, S. L. (2007). *Commentary of Han Fei Zi* (p. 87). Shanghai Bookstore Publishing House.
11. *Analects · Wei Zheng.*
12. Mou, Z. S. (2010).*Way of rule and governance* (p. 29). Student Book.
13. Liang, Q. C. (1982). *The origin of the five nature*. Shanghai Classic Press.
14. Wu, G. Y., Hu, J. W., & Li, X. L. *Note of Guoyu* (p. 21). Shanghai Classic Press.
15. Chen, G. Y. (2007). *The four classics of Emperor Huang* (p. 256). The Commercial Press.
16. There are similar words in Guan Zi·Four Seasons: Yin and Yang are the great principles of heaven and earth. The four seasons are the great manifestations of Yin and Yang. Penalty and virtue harmonize with the four seasons. When penalty and virtue accord with the seasons, they generate blessings; when they contradict, they bring calamity. Virtue corresponds to Yang, penalty corresponds to Yin. Virtue begins in spring and flourishes in summer; penalty begins in autumn and continues through winter.
17. *The Treatise of Feng and Shan*: During the reigns of King Wei and King Xuan of Qi, scholars like Zou Yan and his disciples composed works on the cyclical theory of the Five Virtues. When the Ying Zheng realized the unification, scholars from Qi presented these doctrines to the court, and Ying Zheng adopted them.
18. Fang, X. (2014). *Astrology and law: A study on the cosmological origin and significance of 'modeling heaven' in Ancient Chinese legal tradition* (p. 54). Peking University Press.
19. *Records of the Grand Historian·The Qin Shi Huang.*
20. Qian, M. (1996). *Chinese history* (p. 129). Commercial Press.
21. *Book of Han·Biography of Dong Zhongshu.*
22. *Luxuriant dew of the Spring and Autumn Annals: The correspondence of the four seasons.*

23. Noted by He Xiu in the 9th year of the governance of Xianggong in Zhuan, G. Y. (1980). *The thirteen classics with commentaries and Subcommentaries* (p. 2352). China Publishing House.
24. Noted in the 2nd year of the governance of Yingong in Zhuan, G. Y. (1980). *The thirteen classics with commentaries and subcommentaries* (p. 2202). China Publishing House.
25. *Luxuriant dew of the Spring and Autumn annals: Benevolence and righteousness*.
26. Fuller, L. L. (2007). *The morality of law* (p. 8, Z. Ge, Trans.). The Commercial Press.
27. Huang, J. J. (2006). *The emergence and systematization of Confucianization in traditional Chinese legal system: An analysis based on Cheng Shude's compiled case records of Chunqiu judgment in the Han dynasties* (p. 66). Tsinghua University Press.
28. *Luxuriant dew of the Spring and Autumn Annals: The essence*.
29. *Yan Tie Lun · Virtue and penalty.*
30. Du, Y. (1992). *Tong Dian* (p. 1911). China Publishing House.
31. *Records of the grand historian: Autobiographical postface by the grand scribe.*
32. *Records of the grand historian · Xun Li.*
33. *Book of Han· Dong Zhongshu.*
34. *Book of Han· Xun Li.*
35. Sadao, N. (2004). *The formation and structure of Ancient Chinese empires: A study of the twenty ranks of nobility* (pp. 449–450, W. Shangqing, Trans.). China Publishing House.
36. Zhu, T. (2013). *The classical learning infused into imperial politics: The form and practice of Confucian legal thought in the Han dynasty* (p. 257). China University of Political Science and Law Press.
37. Complete Works of Xiangshan, Volume 22, Miscellaneous Sayings.
38. *The Humble Aspiration Studio collection*, Volume 3, *The duties of a ruler.*
39. *The Humble Aspiration Studio Collection, Volume 2, On the legitimacy of dynastic.*
40. Zhongxin, F. et al. (2006). *Chinese culture and the Chinese legal tradition: Collected legal-historical essays of Chen Guyuan* (p. 99). China University of Political Science and Law Press.

CHAPTER 3

Neither Rule of Virtue nor Rule of Law: The Governance Model of Traditional China

1 "Rule of Virtue" in Ancient China Was Not Simply Virtue Governance

I. Conceptual Analysis of Confucian "Rule of Virtue"

The term "rule of virtue" represents modern scholars' summary of Confucian social governance models, yet its conceptual definition and connotation remain debated. One interpretation views "rule of virtue" as "governing through morality", suggesting social order should primarily be maintained through virtue principles and Confucian values. Another perspective equates "rule of virtue" with "rule by men", arguing that governance relies on virtuous rulers' leadership, where social stability depends entirely on the people's hope for sagacious monarchs. This ruler-dependent model represents typical "rule by men", thus making ancient Confucian "rule of virtue" essentially a form of "rule by man".

Since the establishment of modern rule-of-law principles, scholars have criticized traditional virtue-based governance from the perspective of legal-political philosophy. The most substantial critiques of "rule by virtue" focus on three aspects:

Some critics argue that "rule of virtue" is grounded in a belief in the innate goodness of human nature, thereby lacking institutional safeguards against human natures flaws. Zhang Hao, in his article *The*

D. Li, *Conceptual History of Morality and Penalty in China*, Key Concepts in Chinese Thought and Culture,
https://doi.org/10.1007/978-981-95-9059-9_3

Dim Consciousness and Democratic Tradition, critiques ancient China's "rule of virtue" and "sage-king" tradition. He identifies the fundamental difference between Confucian governance and Western Christian political philosophy as lying in the "the dim consciousness". The Confucian tradition maintains that all humans possess the potential for virtue perfection, believing that politics led by virtuous "sage-kings" constitutes the key to harmonious society. Thus, Confucianism holds that political power should be transformed through inner virtue cultivation rather than constrained through external institutions [1]. Although Zhang acknowledges certain "dim consciousness" in Confucianism regarding human fallibility, and recognizes its strong critical spirit through virtue evaluations of rulers, he identifies three characteristics in the Mencius-Xunzi developed "sage-king" model: First, an "ultimate optimistic spirit" believing humans can achieve virtue perfection and divine connection; second, a tendency toward fuse politics and moral instruction, where "sage-kings" serve as both "being the parent of his people" and "the conduit of the Way for the world"; third, a utopian inclination embedded in this optimistic spirit [2]. Zhang's critique is particularly incisive, as his three characteristics of the "sage-king" model seemingly demonstrate Confucian "rule of virtue" fundamental incompatibility with modern democratic politics.

One critique holds that the practice of "rule of virtue", both historically and in contemporary times, implies a blurred boundary between law and virtue, leading to the issue of virtue legalization. Sun Li critiques both the ancient tradition of "rule of virtue" and its current practice in China from a legal-philosophical perspective on the relationship between law and virtue. She argues that traditional "rule of virtue" inevitably encounters three problems in governance: First, the comprehensive affirmation of virtue in legislation, which commonly understood as the issue of virtue legalization; second, the characteristic of "punishing the heart", where an entirely ethicized law regulates not only behavior but also beliefs and thoughts; third, the individualization and hierarchical nature of justice, where judicial decisions based on sentiment undermine the certainty and predictability of the law. Thus, she asserts that the rule of law holds legitimacy compared to "rule of virtue", as it ensures not only just outcomes but also procedural justice. Regarding contemporary "rule of virtue" practices, she contends that so-called virtue construction should, in essence, be "the institutional construction of a virtue environment" [3].

Some argue that "rule of virtue", relying on Confucian ethical values to legitimize the ruler, conflates public morality and private morality, while lacking effective institutional constraints. Jiang Yihua, a scholar from Taiwan province of China, compares Confucian "rule of virtue" with Max Weber's typology of political legitimacy and concludes that Confucian "rule of virtue" does not fit any of Weber's three types of legitimacy. Instead, he proposes that Confucian "rule of virtue" represents a hybrid "morality-based domination" model. His critique of Confucian "rule of virtue" centers on two points: First, the legitimacy of a ruler under moral domination cannot be effectively constrained by institutions; second, the "filial piety and fraternal duty"-centered "rule of virtue" blurs the boundary between public and private. The principal merit of Jiang's work lies in his critique of "rule of virtue" from the perspective of the public–private distinction. He points out that the primary ethical value in Confucian "rule of virtue" is "filial piety and fraternal duty", which is unsuitable as a basis for governance in the public sphere [4].

The three aforementioned critiques of Confucian "rule of virtue" represent prevailing academic perspectives that reflect common understandings and criticisms of this governance model. However, upon examining the historical development of Confucian thought regarding the virtue-punishment relationship, we find these critiques contain varying degrees of misinterpretation.

Liang Qichao's interpretation of "rule of virtue" proves particularly insightful in clarifying these modern misunderstandings. Contrary to the view that Confucians naively placed political hopes on virtuous rulers' benevolent governance, Liang argued: "The Confucians firmly believed that sound politics cannot exist without sound citizens. Therefore, their political philosophy focused solely on cultivating political morality, capability, and habits among the majority" [5]. Here, Liang essentially elucidates the meaning of "rule of virtue" from the perspective of moral autonomy. The Confucian advocacy of ritual-music education aimed to develop fundamental virtue qualities among the people, enabling each individual acquire basic cultivation and become a sound citizen. With morally cultivated citizens, there would be no need for sagely monarchs as helmsmen or leaders to interfere in people's lives, nor for threats of punishment or political oppression and good political order would emerge naturally. Liang maintained that Confucian expectations of virtuous rulers concerned only virtue transformation, which in his view also implied civic self-governance. He stated: “While Confucians did hope for sage-monarchs and worthy ministers, their hope lay not in governing the people or managing affairs, but in transforming the people and perfecting customs’” [6]. Therefore, Liang understood the core of Confucian “rule by men” or “rule of virtue” as cultivating political morality among all citizens, what we now call civic virtue. Far from contradicting democracy, this approach actually constituted progress toward democratic ideals.

Building upon Liang Qichao’s interpretation of Confucian “rule of virtue”, we can analyze the concept and essence of Confucian governance in the following three aspects to respond to current academic criticisms:

First, Confucian “rule of virtue” should not be simplistically understood as “governance by virtue” It does not mean administering state affairs solely based on Confucian virtue principles or ethical values. Regarding pre-Qin Confucian thought, Confucians did not disregard the significance of law. The Confucian concept of “rite” essentially functioned as the law of ancient society, encompassing not only “civil law” that regulated social order but more importantly serving as fundamental constitutional principles governing state politics. As some scholars have noted: “In the Chinese legal tradition, rite held the status of fundamental law, unchanging by rulers’ preferences, rooted in popular consciousness, serving as the supreme legal standard above ordinary laws that judged all rights and wrongs” [7]. In reality, there was never a historical period in ancient China where virtue served as the primary governance tool. Even during the Western Zhou Dynasty that advocated “illustrating virtue and cautious punishment”, rulers still attached great importance to the role of punishment. As accurately summarized in the early Spring and Autumn period: “*The Book of Zhou* states: ‘Illustrate virtue and cautious punishment’ was King Wen’s foundation for establishing Zhou. Illustrating virtue means elevating it; cautious punishment means eliminating crimes” [8]. Here, “cautious punishment” not only advocated leniency and prudence in sentencing, but more importantly stressed punishment’s functional value in sanctioning crimes and misconduct to eradicate social ills, hence the meaning of “eliminating”. If we simplistically interpret Confucian “rule of virtue” as “governing through morality”, we encounter the paradox noted by legal historians: “While the book *History of Chinese Legal Thought* present ‘virtue given priority over penalty’ as the guiding principle of Chinese legal tradition, *History of Chinese Legal System* characterize ancient Chinese law as ‘penal-focused’ and ‘emphasizing criminal over civil law’”[7].

Secondly, the primary method of Confucian "rule of virtue" lies in "moral transformation". Xu Fuguan argued that the concepts of "rule of virtue" and "education" are fundamentally inseparable. He maintained: "Confucius' notion of political non-action ultimately sought to replace governance with education. This represents the core content of rule of virtue". The substitution of governance with education constitutes the key to understanding Confucian "rule of virtue" [9]. As Mencius stated in *Jinxin II*: "Good governance secures people's wealth; good education wins their hearts". This educational approach was specifically proposed as an alternative to the Legalist "rule of punishment". While Legalist governance relied on state coercion, Confucius advocated "guiding through virtue", using virtue education to alleviate political pressure. Some scholars worry that Confucian virtue education through "those above setting examples for those below" might lead to rulers forcibly imposing virtue, blurring public–private boundaries, and eliminating individual freedom. Yet this criticism proves unfounded—how could Confucianism, which consistently upholds the "way of faithfulness and reciprocity", endorse such coercive imposition? As the Analects state: "The gentleman does not reproach others for what they cannot do, nor shame them for their limitations" [10]. In reality, far from demanding universal adherence to sage-like standards, Confucianism explicitly opposed compulsory virtue education. This explains Confucianism's differentiated standards for self-cultivation versus governing others. *The Book of Rites* articulates this principle: "The gentleman deliberates the Way for himself, but establishes laws according to the people's capacity". Here, the "Way" for self-deliberation represents the rigorous standards of self-cultivation toward sagehood, strictly self-imposed requirements. "Establishing laws for the people" means formulating social norms based on achievable everyday ethics for ordinary people—the "Doctrine of the Mean". Dong Zhongshu further elaborated: "Inward governance returns to principle to rectify oneself, following rite to cultivate blessings. Outward governance extends kindness broadly, applying lenient measures to accommodate all. Therefore, to govern others by self-discipline's strictness shows ungenerous leadership. To self-govern by others' standards shows ritual disrespect" [11]. Clearly, Confucian maintains strict self-discipline while exercising in virtue expectations toward others.

Finally, the ultimate objective of Confucian "rule of virtue" is to enable the people's "self-transformation" and to realize communal self-governance. Mou Zongsan argued that the fundamental function of "rule of virtue" lies in awakening people's virtue consciousness, making them ashamed of wrongdoing and inclined toward goodness. More importantly, Mou maintained: "The highest and ultimate realm of Confucian virtue transformation in governance is 'each rectifying their inherent nature'. From its inception, virtuous governance regards each individual as an end in themselves—through moral awakening, they can strive upward and fulfill their potential" [12]. In Mou's view, Confucian "virtue transformation" was never about rulers' condescending virtue preaching, but rather about inspiring people's virtue self-awareness through education.

In summary, Confucian "rule of virtue" does not represent simplistic moral politics, but rather a comprehensive social governance model of "taking virtue and rite as foundation while supplementing with administration and punishment". It encompasses two main dimensions: First, it emphasizes political "virtue". Confucianism provides legitimacy criteria for actual governance through its ideal "kingly way" politics, clarifying hierarchical relationships between ruler and ministers through "rectification of names", stressing that each should fulfill their proper roles with corresponding virtues. Second, Confucianism advocates governing society through virtue education, transforming customs and cultural patterns through pervasive, diffuse Confucian cultivation that influences social and political actions. Unlike the coercive methods of Legalist "rule of punishment", Confucian virtue education emphasizes cultural transformation, focusing on subtly reshaping behavior by internalizing legal norms and social ethics as tacit knowledge in daily life through the exemplary and pedagogical roles of scholar-gentlemen in local communities.

II. The Political Value and Implementation Methods of Confucian "Rule of Virtue"

1. Confucian "Virtue" Transformed Traditional Politics from "Divine" to "Human" Orientation

In early Chinese society, law and divine will were inextricably linked—a period modern scholars call the "Divine Law Period", primarily referring primarily to the Xia, Shang, and Western Zhou Dynasties, collectively known as the "Three Dynasties" in ancient discourse. While reliable historical materials about the Xia Dynasty remain scarce, fragments in *the Book of Documents* reveal that rulers believed their authority derived from heavenly mandate, viewing law as an instrument for administering divine punishment. Not only law but ancient rites (li) also possessed a profound religious and mystical character. The origin and core of primordial rite lay in ancestral veneration and sacrificial worship, as encapsulated in the axiom: "Of the five classical rites, none surpasses sacrifice in importance" [13]. Scholar Wang Guowei's etymological analysis of the ancient character for "rite" traces its origins to rituals serving deities: "Vessels holding jade for worshipping spirits were called feng; by extension, the wine offered to divine beings was called li; further extended, all services for spirits became known as "Li" (rite)" [14]. This demonstrates that China's early institutional norms of rite evolved from tribal sacrificial practices, representing continuations of religious proto-rituals.

The emergence of the concept of "virtue" fundamentally broke the divine nature of early Chinese law. The Western Zhou's doctrine of "matching heaven with virtue" developed this synthesis of heavenly will and political morality, marking a crucial transition where celestial mandate alone could no longer sufficiently legitimize legal authority. Political legitimacy became contingent upon popular sentiment. Rulers had to govern conscientiously and prioritize human affairs to maintain the Mandate of Heaven. This early conception of virtue liberated law from divine systems based on "inscrutable heavenly principles", enabling the recognition of inherent human value and agency. As "virtue" became the dominant discourse for articulating political legitimacy, both law and rites gradually emancipated themselves from religious determinism and supernatural constraints, fostering more rational and mature political philosophy. The Western Zhou emphasis on "Respecting Virtue to Protect the Populace" made popular welfare the essential criterion of political virtue, establishing a "people-centered" governance ideal. Particularly after Confucians developed "rule of virtue" theory, the kingly way principle of "Protect the People and then Rule as a King" became the paramount standard for political legitimacy. Through this philosophical evolution, both legal and ritual systems completed their transformation from divine to human-centered foundations.

From the perspective of intellectual history, it was during the flourishing period of Confucianism that the rites, originally permeated with religious character, underwent a genuine humanistic transformation. Through Confucius' interpretation, Confucian humanism became profoundly embedded within traditional ritual systems. The conceptual vehicle for this humanization process was precisely Confucius' formulation of "humaneness".

The Master achieved the perfect synthesis of ritual and humaneness by interpreting "rite" through the lens of "humaneness" and practicing "humaneness" through the observance of "rites", as encapsulated in the dictum: "To discipline oneself and return to the rites constitutes humaneness". Confucius traced the Zhou ritual of "three-year mourning" directly to the natural affection between parent and child, thereby grounding the entire ritual system's consanguineous core in "filial piety", while simultaneously basing filial piety itself on the simple, everyday love between parents and children. Consequently, the practice of traditional rites came to depend on inner psychological disposition rather than external coercion, much less religious mysticism. It was precisely by establishing this foundation in ordinary human psychology that rite became truly humanized. Their justification and legitimacy now wholly derived from human nature itself.

In summary, Confucianism fundamentally shifted the foundation of traditional Chinese social norms from the divine to the human realm. A transformation of epoch-making significance in Chinese legal history that shaped the distinctive characteristic of "reasonableness and human sentiment" characteristic of traditional Chinese law. This constitutes one of the most profound differences between Chinese and Western legal traditions. By grounding the legitimacy of social norms directly in lived experience rather than divine will, Confucius established Chinese traditional law's rationality upon psychological and emotional foundations, thereby creating the conceptual space for interaction between state law, natural principles, and human feelings. As the Qing Dynasty legal expert Wang Huizu insightfully observed: "While mastering legal texts is important, the true art of legal application lies in skillfully embodying human sentiment" [15]. Here, "human sentiment" refers precisely to the Confucian ethical relationships of "Father's Kindness and Son's filial piety", "husband's righteousness and wife's compliance", and "friendliness and respect among brothers" Thus, we see the humanistic elements of traditional Chinese law manifested in these kinship-based principles of reasonableness and emotion.

2. Confucian "Rule of Virtue" Provided Normative Foundations for Political Legitimacy

The essence of "rule of virtue" lies in whether rulers can first cultivate their own virtue, requiring them to possess the moral qualities necessary for governance. Confucian "good teaching" shares this same fundamental premise, first demanding that rulers develop essential virtues. This virtue standard for rulers constitutes what might be called "rectifying the ruler" from the perspective of virtuous governance, or "self-rectification" from the perspective of moral education. As Mencius stated in *Lilou I*: "Only great men can rectify what is wrong in the ruler's mind". Zhu Xi's commentary explains: "Great men are those of great virtue who rectify themselves and thereby rectify others" [16]. This reveals the relationship between self-rectification and ruler-rectification. "rectification of the ruler" is achieved precisely through the ruler's own "self-rectification" to "correct what is wrong in his mind". This philosophy is equally expressed in the Analects: "Governing means rectifying. When you lead by rectitude, who would dare not be rectified?" [17] and "Governing through virtue is like the North Star. It remains in its place while all other stars revolve around it" [18]. Both passages articulate this central Confucian principle.

The fundamental distinction between political power and brute violence lies in the former's necessary precondition of legitimacy. Western natural law theorists have primarily engaged in examining the legitimacy of political power and legal systems themselves—what Lon Fuller termed "The Morality of Law" essentially constitutes the requirement that laws must satisfy moral criteria of legitimacy. The inquiry into the legitimate operation of political power represents a shared concern across Chinese and Western intellectual traditions, with ancient Chinese thinkers persistently grappling with this very question. In traditional Chinese thought, concepts like the "Mandate of Heaven" or Laozi's "Dao" served as transcendent standards for evaluating the legitimacy of secular political power. Among these traditions, Confucian political philosophy exhibited the most systematic concern with legitimacy issues, establishing criteria based on "people-centered" principles—far more discernible than the Yin-Yang School's mystical and ineffable celestial will. Within Confucianism, Mencius developed the most sophisticated framework for political legitimacy. His entire philosophical system essentially revolves around rendering political power's exercise more legitimate. The core of Mencian thought, benevolent governance, simultaneously provides criteria for the legitimate exercise of monarchical power. What Mencius called "rectifying the ruler" meant regulating the sovereign's conduct and authority, thereby establishing legitimate foundations for power's proper use. For Mencius, while political authority derived from "heaven's conferral and the people's consent", celestial will remained inscrutable and popular sentiment difficult to ascertain in pre-democratic eras. He therefore identified the implementation of benevolent governance as the paramount criterion for political legitimacy.

Mencius believed that the ruler's authority was bestowed by Heaven, while simultaneously entailing a fiduciary relationship between the ruler and the people. Mencius once used the analogy of entrusting his wife to a friend during his absence, pointing out that if the friend failed in this duty and left his wife cold and hungry, such a friendship would be unworthy of existence. By the same logic, if a ruler failed to protect and enrich the people, their rule would lack legitimacy [19]. Therefore, the ruler must diligently practice benevolent governance to ensure the people's welfare. In this way, benevolent governance becomes intrinsically linked to the legitimacy of political power, serving as the criterion for judging political legitimacy.

2 Endogenous Social Order Is the Ideal Form of "Rule of Virtue"

I. The Opposition Between Two Perspectives on Social Order

Since modern times, there have been two different perspectives on the formation of social order in the philosophical field. One perspective holds that social order is a natural outcome of human behavior, believing that the social order of human society spontaneously emerges from human actions. The other perspective argues that order is a product of human rationality and is consciously designed. Hayek referred to these two types of order as "artificial order" originating from external arrangements and "spontaneous order" emerging from internal self-growth. Hayek stated, "There exist in society a great many ordered structures which are the product of the actions of many men but are not the result of human design" [20]. Corresponding to these two types of order is the distinction between internal rules and external rules. Internal rules generally refer to private law rules in a broad sense, while external rules mainly refer to the rules of general social organizations with a public law nature. Internal rules constitute a spontaneous order, while external rules constitute an artificial order. Hayek believed that only internal rules are law in the strict sense. He said, internal rules can prevent conflicts between the actions of individuals by enabling each individual and group to be aware of the consequences of their actions and demarcate inviolable personal spheres for individuals. Internal rules are abstract and independent of individual purposes, and they form a spontaneous or internal order that is equal, abstract, and goal-independent [21].

Thus, how is this spontaneous order and its internal rules constituted, and how are they followed by people? Hayek posits that although people may not articulate the "spontaneous rules" governing social order, they possess an innate "tacit knowledge" of these norms. Compliance with such rules does not necessitate a rationalized, explicit understanding of their underlying principles [22]. Hayek illustrates this concept through quotidian activities such as artisanal craftsmanship and cycling, wherein practitioners rely on "practical know-how"—a form of inarticulate expertise that resists formal codification. This notion of "tacit knowledge" bears a striking resemblance to the Confucian conception of social order. Confucianism maintains that the observance of norms among the populace is cultivated through the subtle exemplification and moral edification of the literati. Hence, the teachings of the sages are such that the common people "The people may be made to follow, but must not be made to know why". Moreover, Confucian moral precepts are not devised from the abstract ethical ideals of sages but are rooted in the practicable virtues of everyday life. These norms neither seek to rectify human nature nor aspire to transcend it. Ordinary individuals instinctively adhere to Confucian ethics in their daily conduct, guided by an innate virtue intuition. Yet, as laypersons, they seldom engage in conscious reflection upon the philosophical foundations of these norms—a phenomenon encapsulated in the adage, "The people may be made to follow, but must not be made to know why". In traditional Chinese society, compliance with communal norms largely operated through this mechanism of "tacit knowledge". State laws and customary practices were observed without reliance on formal promulgation by magistrates or local gentry; the populace appeared to intuit the legal parameters governing civil affairs and regulated their conduct accordingly. As elucidated by Shuzo Shiga in his analysis of positive law and custom in traditional Chinese jurisprudence: "In domains such as familial relations, where affective bonds ostensibly supersede legal formalism, what proves remarkable is the clarity with which individuals recognize their respective entitlements, resolving disputes through shared normative understandings. Thus, even in the absence of codified statutes, an unwritten juridical logic, deeply embedded in collective consciousness and operative in practice, may be termed 'legal consciousness', or analogously, 'natural law.'" [23] Shiga's "legal consciousness" corresponds to what may be described as a "cultural paradigm"—a framework wherein Confucian ethics and statutory laws were synthesized through moral acculturation. Governed by this paradigm, individuals voluntarily conformed to legal stipulations. The Confucian ideal of "rule of virtue" resides precisely in this harmonization of ethical norms and state mandates, transmuted into the populace's "tacit knowledge" via pedagogical osmosis, thereby ensuring the organic fulfillment of legal obligations in quotidian life.

The Confucian concept of "rule of virtue" encompasses not only the everyday ethics of the people but also systematically codifies these daily norms and folk customs into state law. As the Confucianization of law progressed, state laws incorporated more Confucian ethical norms, while Confucian ethics and rites became increasingly legalized. From a substantive perspective, Confucian virtue education in civil society served not only to exemplify ethical norms but also functioned as legal pedagogy. Through the imperceptible virtue influence, the state's coercive legal framework was disseminated via ethical acculturation, aligning popular conduct spontaneously with statutory requirements. Consequently, the external order imposed by state coercion was internalized through Confucian virtue transformation, becoming a self-regulated internal order observed voluntarily by the people.

II. The Confucian Ideal of Social Organization

Our preceding discussion has elucidated the Confucian governance approach of synthesizing state decrees with its ethical system, ultimately transforming them into societal "tacit knowledge" to achieve social self-governance. The Confucian approach to virtue transformation operates through two fundamental mechanisms: One is to construct the entire political and legal system based on ethical relational order, so that the state's mandatory normative system is consistent with the interpersonal relationship structure in society. The political and legal system built on the foundation of human relational order coordinates state laws and decrees with the daily ethics related to human relations that are well-known to the common people in their daily lives. This helps internalize the state's mandatory normative system into a self-generating and endogenous social order. Secondly, Confucianism has shaped the ideal personality image of junzi who can coordinate human relational order and consciously practice Confucian ethics. Confucianism hopes that through the exemplary influence, junzi can morally enlighten the common people in civil society through their own actions, transforming state laws and decrees that embody human relational order into the "tacit knowledge" of the people. At the same time, junzi can also serve as a link to coordinate civil order and bridge the gap between officials and the people, playing a crucial role in the formation of a spontaneous order in civil society. The following is a detailed discussion of these two important aspects of the basic logic of Confucian "virtualization".

On the one hand, when designing the political structure, Confucianism took human relational order as the foundation for maintaining the entire social relations and political mechanisms. As Mencius articulated in explicating his vision of benevolent governance: "When those are thus illustrated by superiors, kindly feeling will prevail among the inferior people below. Should a real sovereign arise, he will certainly come and take an example from you; and thus you will be the teacher of the true sovereign" [24]. This demonstrates how Mencius invoked the precedent of the Three Dynasties, all of which prioritized clarifying ethical relationships, to establish that contemporary rulers pursuing benevolent governance must similarly adhere to this paradigm. The Confucian ideal of rule of virtue essentially constructs social order through the systematic clarification of interpersonal ethics, with the Five Cardinal Relationships serving as its foundational framework. Following the era of a unified empire, Confucianism incorporated the Legalist doctrine of Three Cardinal Guides, thereby transforming the originally reciprocal ethical relationships into a legally codified hierarchy centered on authoritarian principles.

On the other hand, junzi serves as the link in the Confucian rule of virtue, bridging the ruler and the people and uniting common social values. Confucius' conceptualization of junzi's social role and virtue character essentially established a rational criterion for the ancient patriarchal system, envisioning morally cultivated gentlemen as societal stewards. "When Zilu asked how to be a superior man, the Master said, 'Cultivate yourself to foster a sincere manner.' 'Is that all?' asked Zilu. 'Cultivate yourself so as to bring peace and happiness to other people,' replied the

Master" [25]. As Hsiao Kung-chuan observed: "Thus Confucius' ideal junzi achieves virtue and position through merit, neither relying solely on hereditary privilege like clan patriarchs, nor seizing power through force like usurpers. The former may be legal but not necessarily legitimate; the latter violates both principle and law". In terms of purpose, Confucius's ideal actually lies in "recreating the ruling class for the feudal world" [26]. From a contemporary jurisprudential perspective, Confucius' vision of "virtue legitimizing position" essentially established an ethical criterion for political legitimacy. His concern centered on the virtue dimensions of power: the qualifications of power-holders, the requisite virtues of governance, and the ethical foundations of political institutions and perennial questions addressed through his ideal of junzi governance. The Confucian *junzi* (Man of Virtue) represents a class of virtuous local gentry and social elites thoroughly imbued with Confucian ethics. Their significance lies not merely in possessing moral virtue, but more crucially in its practical implementation. The Confucian requirements for a *junzi*'s (Man of Virtue) conduct carry profound sociopolitical implications, particularly regarding public administration. Through personal cultivation and embodiment of Confucian ethics, *junzi* (Man of Virtue) becomes a paradigmatic figure for local communities, thereby advancing virtue development and social governance. The famous sequence of "Self-Cultivation, Family Regulation, State Governance, Bringing Peace to All Under Heaven" encapsulates the Confucian ideal: through gradual ethical actualization, *junzi* (Man of Virtue) facilitates societal transformation toward the ultimate political vision of universal harmony.

3 The Traditional Chinese Understanding of the Relationship Between Virtue and Rule of Law

The Chinese philosophical concept of "virtue" constitutes a multidimensional construct with nuanced interpretations across various discursive contexts. This examination shall confine itself to the Confucian conceptualization of virtue, with particular emphasis on its semantic parameters within the contemporary academic framework of "virtue given priority over penalty". Analytical scrutiny reveals that pre-Qin Confucianism articulated the notion of virtue through two principal dimensions: the political and the personal. In political dimension, it manifests through three distinct yet interrelated concepts: virtuous governance, rule of virtue, and virtue education. Virtuous governance denotes the virtue legitimacy of sovereign authority. Confucian doctrine establishes its theoretical foundations through: The paradigm of benevolent governance and the principle of nominal rectification. The former serving as the normative political ideal and providing evaluative criteria for existing regimes; the latter preserving political virtue through the clarification of reciprocal obligations between sovereign and minister, thereby ensuring proper adherence to respective roles and ethical conduct. Rule of virtue and virtue education have a relationship of purpose and means. In terms of governance models, governance through virtue represents the institutional framework, while virtue cultivation constitutes its operational mechanism. The personal dimension of virtue pertains to the ethical qualities incumbent upon individuals to cultivate. Confucian philosophy postulates that: virtue is inherent in human nature and remains universally accessible irrespective of social stratification. It manifests differentially according to social position: magisterial virtue for rulers and civic virtue for individuals. The Confucian system prioritizes: the inculcation of magisterial virtue among rulers to implement governance through virtue suasion and the cultivation of civic virtue through pedagogical means to foster autonomous ethical regulation among the individuals. This dual cultivation aims to achieve a state of "governing through non-action", thereby minimizing disruptive coercive intervention in the normal order of communal life.

The conceptual disparity between ancient and modern notions of "law" presents a complex issue. The traditional Chinese conception of "law" differs fundamentally from its Western counterpart. Indeed, as Professor Zhu Suli metaphorically observed, the distinction between Chinese and Western "law" is not merely one between varieties of apples, but like comparing bananas and oranges [27]. What is termed "law" in modern times could refer to multiple normative concepts in ancient China. Mr. Yan Fu recognized this problem when translating Montesquieu's *The Spirit of the Laws*. He noted: "The Western term 'law' may correspond to four distinct Chinese concepts—rite, principle, statutes, and institutions—which scholars must carefully discern", and further explained that "what Western texts call 'law' actually encompasses China's ritual codes" [28]. Although Yan Fu's discussion focused on the Sino-Western conceptual differences of "law", China's legal modernization since the late Qing Dynasty's legal reforms has essentially been a process of Westernization. Consequently, the modern Chinese conception of "law" predominantly inherits the Western legal tradition. Thus, the contemporary distinction between ancient and modern Chinese "law" concepts mirrors what Yan Fu described as the difference between Chinese and Western notions. Expanding upon Yan Fu's thesis, we can identify three primary distinctions between ancient and modern "law" concepts: First, divergence in Conceptual Scope. The modern "law" incorporates the distinction between positive law and natural law. In contrast, ancient Chinese "law" primarily referred to normative decrees issued by the state, manifested in various legal forms such as disciplines, ordinances, regulations, rules, precedents, or codes. What modern jurisprudence considers natural law was, in the ancient view, largely embodied in "principle" or "ritual propriety" [29]. Second, differences in manifestation. Previous scholarship, viewing ancient law through a modern lens, has offered many interpretations highlighting the ancient-modern divide—for instance, characterizing ancient law as predominantly codified, and emphasizing "penal-centric, undifferentiated civil-criminal" features. Such interpretations often overlook the representational differences between ancient and modern law. The ancient conception included not only codified state institutions like statutes and codes, but also rite, regarded as the foundation of the traditional legal system, alongside numerous quasi-legal village covenants and clan rules. Third, variation in regulatory methods. Ancient law primarily governed social relations through rewards and punishments, with historical legal codes placing greater emphasis on the latter. Consequently, examining only the law of ancient societies easily leads to the conclusion that the Chinese legal tradition was "penal-centric".

Regarding the relationship between virtue and law, when examined through the lens of ancient Chinese conceptions of "law", their interplay in traditional society often manifested as a dialectical tension and complementary dynamic between "virtue" and "punishment". As previously discussed, virtue and punishment frequently appeared as paired antithetical concepts, particularly in *Zuo Zhuan*, where they were juxtaposed to emphasize their equally indispensable roles in governance. For instance, *Zuo Zhuan* defines their relationship thus: "To quell rebellion is the function of punishment; to pacify submission is the function of virtue" [30]. "Virtue restrains wickedness; punishment suppresses disorder. Where neither virtue nor punishment is established, wickedness and disorder will arise together" [31]. In this framework, virtue and punishment stand in opposition: Virtue operates through methods of "appeasement", "conciliation", and "leniency"—employing benevolent means to pacify the people. Punishment, by contrast, employs methods of "subjugation", "suppression", and "deterrence"—relying on coercive force to crush rebellion. It was precisely through the Spring and Autumn period thinkers' reflections on the distinct political logics of virtue and punishment that later generations developed the philosophy of "emphasizing both virtue and punishment" or "balancing leniency and severity". The strategic principle of "alternating civil and martial governance", which traces its roots to the hegemonic strategies of the Spring and Autumn era that juxtaposed virtue and punishment. Through the intellectual debates between Confucians and Legalists during the pre-Qin period, virtue and punishment gradually evolved into two opposing models of governance: Confucian virtue-based governance and Legalist punishment-centric rule.

It should be noted that the ancient Confucian concept of "virtue" carried different connotations depending on context. However, when contrasted with "punishment", "virtue" primarily referred to "virtue-based governance" as a mode of social administration that stood in opposition to the Legalist "rule of punishment". Thus, the "virtue-punishment" duality in the classical principle of "virtue given priority over penalty" does not simply denote an opposition between "virtue versus penalties", or "leniency versus severity" as governance techniques. Rather, it represents a hierarchical relationship between two governance paradigms: the Confucian "rule of virtue" served as the dominant framework, while selectively incorporating practical institutional measures from Legalist punishment-centric approaches. Examining traditional Chinese governance through this lens reveals that "virtue" and "punishment" maintained an ontological hierarchy of "essence-function": Confucian virtue governance shaped the core values, spirit, and fundamental models of traditional Chinese politics and law, whereas the rational elements of the Legalist "rule of punishment" were adopted as pragmatic means (*yong*) for specific governance needs.

Contemporary scholarship commonly characterizes the relationship between Confucianism and Legalism in the political framework of imperial China as "Taking Legalism in the name of Confucianism". This formulation has been interpreted in two predominant ways: the state ostensibly embodied Confucian benevolent governance, while its actual operations followed Legalist authoritarian principles. Or, Confucianism shaped societal ethics, whereas Legalism constituted the institutional ethos [32]. However, through our examination of the institutional implementation of the Confucian principle "virtue given priority over penalty", we propose a necessary reinterpretation. The core institutional spirit and fundamental governance framework of traditional China were fundamentally molded by Confucian's rule of virtue. Virtue served as the ultimate criterion for political legitimacy and institutional rationality. While, the externalization of virtue through ritual norms directly constituted: the foundational spirit of traditional Chinese law and the political architecture of imperial governance.

Bibliography

1. Hao, Z. (2006). *The democratic tradition and the consciousness of darkness* (p. 12). Linking Publishing.
2. Hao, Z. (2006). *The democratic tradition and the consciousness of darkness* (p. p97). Linking Publishing.
3. Li, S. (2002). *An analysis of the legitimacy of rule of virtue and rule of law: With reflections on Chinese and East Asian legal-cultural traditions. Social Sciences in China, 6.*
4. Chiang, Y. -H. (2008). The political concepts and their characteristics in the *analects of confucius. Review of Political and Social Philosophy, 24.*
5. Qichao, L. (2004). *History of pre-Qin political thought* (p. 98). Tianjin Ancient Books Publishing House.
6. Qichao, L. (2004). *History of pre-Qin political thought* (p. 99). Tianjin Ancient Books Publishing House.
7. Ma, X. (2014). Clarifying the relationship between 'rite' and 'law' in the Chinese legal system: Questioning certain 'established conclusions' in Chinese legal history research. *Chinese Journal of Law, 1.*
8. *Zuo Zhuan: The second year of Duke Cheng.*
9. Fuguan, X. (2002). *A detailed exegesis of Confucius's thought on rule of virtue*, c*ollected essays on the history of Chinese thought* (p. 221). Student Book Co., Ltd.
10. *Book of rite: The record on example.*
11. *Luxuriant gems of the Spring and Autumn annals: Methods of benevolence and righteousness (No. 29).*
12. Zongsan, M. (2010). *The way of politics and the way of governance* (p. 29). Student Book Co., Ltd.
13. *Book of rites: The meaning of sacrifices.*
14. Guowei, W. (1959). *An exegesis of "Li", Guantang Collection* (p. 291). Zhonghua Book Company.

15. *Admonitions on governance : Curbing litigation.*
16. Xi, Z. (1983). *Collected commentaries on the four books* (p. 285). Zhonghua Book Company.
17. *The analects: Yan Yuan.*
18. *The analects: Wei Zheng.*
19. *Mencius: Liang Hui Wang II.*
20. von Hayek, F. A. (2003). *Law, legislation and liberty* (Vol. 1, p. 55, D. Zhenglai, Trans.). Encyclopedia of China Publishing House.
21. Hayek. (1978). *New studies in philosophy, politics, economics and the history of ideas* (p. 77). Routledge & Kegan Paul.
22. von Hayek, F. A. (1997). *The constitution of liberty* (Vol. 1, p. 22, D. Zhenglai, Trans.). SDX Joint Publishing Company.
23. Shuzo, S. (2002). *The principle of Chinese family law* (p. 10). Law Press.
24. *Mencius: Teng Wen Gong I.*
25. *The analects: Xian Wen.*
26. Gongquan, X. (2010). *A history of Chinese political thought* (p. 48). New Star Press.
27. Li, S. (1998). *The story of law, Reading* (No. 7).
28. Fu, Y. (1981). *The spirit of the laws by Montesquieu* (pp. 3, 7). The Commercial Press.
29. Xianyi, Z., & Xiaohong, M. (2003). *The structure and basic concepts of traditional Chinese law: On the relationship between ancient rite and law. Social Sciences in China, 5.*
30. *Zuo Zhuan: The twelfth year of Duke Xuan.*
31. *Zuo Zhuan: The seventeen year of Duke Cheng.*
32. Xiaobo, W. (2015). Confucianism in appearance, legalism in essence" represents the mainstream of Chinese culture. *Guangming Daily.*

CHAPTER 4

Virtue Given Priority over Punishment: A Modern Misconception?

1 The "Virtue Given Priority over Penalty" Theory in the Context of "Rule of Virtue vs. Rule of Law" Discourse

I. The Reduction of Confucian Political-Legal Thought to "Rule of Virtue Doctrine"

Modern scholars studying the history of ancient Chinese thought often adopt Western concepts and frameworks to evaluate and analyze ancient Chinese figures and ideas. Some have vividly likened this research approach to "viewing antiquities under the glow of foreign goods" [1]. By observing and measuring ancient Chinese thought through a Western lens while simultaneously drawing forced parallels between Chinese ideas and Western concepts, this trend has directly contributed to the emergence of a discourse that pits "rule of law" against "rule of virtue" as opposing paradigms. Liang Qichao exemplified this tendency in his work *History of Pre-Qin Political Thought*, where he classified pre-Qin political philosophies into four categories: Daoist "rule through non-action", Confucian "rule by men", also termed "rule of virtue" or "rule of rite", Mohist "rule by divine will" and Legalist "rule of law" or "rule by object". Liang's classification, particularly his framing of Confucian "rule of virtue/rite" as "rule by men" in opposition to Legalist "rule of law",

D. Li, *Conceptual History of Morality and Penalty in China*, Key Concepts in Chinese Thought and Culture,
https://doi.org/10.1007/978-981-95-9059-9_4

has profoundly influenced subsequent intellectual and academic circles, especially legal studies [2]. For instance, Wang Zhenxian, a jurist of the Republican era, further promoted this binary in *Ancient Chinese Jurisprudence*. He enthusiastically endorsed Legalist thought as embodying "rule of law", even listing figures like Zhuge Liang and Fu Jian as advocates. The inevitable corollary was his critique of Confucian "rule by men" and "rule of virtue". Wang attributed China's perceived underdevelopment of legal institutions solely to the "exclusive worship of Confucianism", condemning not only Confucian governance theories but also Han Dynasty legal commentaries for "merely engaging in literal interpretations, utterly divorced from the original spirit of the Warring States Legalists" [3].

However, it was another modern legal historian, Qu Tongzu, who truly amplified Liang Qichao's dichotomy between "rule of virtue" and "rule of law", exerting a profound influence on a century of legal-historical scholarship. In *Law and Society of China*, Qu offered this critique of Confucian "rule of virtue":

> The Confucians firmly believed that human virtue or depravity was determined by virtue education, while simultaneously maintaining that such education depended entirely on the transformative influence of one or two rulers whose charismatic virtue possessed extraordinary power to inspire. Thus, the doctrine of 'rule of virtue' inevitably evolved into 'rule by men'. While 'rule of virtue' refers to the process of virtue transformation, 'rule by men' emphasizes the virtue exemplar themselves—two sides of the same coin [4].

From Qu's perspective, Confucian "rule of virtue" found its expression in "virtue education", implemented exclusively by the ruling class. The crux of this indoctrination lay in the supreme ruler's exceptional virtue charisma, which: imposed ethical demands on rulers and implicitly endorsed the notion that a ruler who rigorously upheld virtue standards could legitimately consolidate political authority and moral leadership into absolutist power. Unquestionably, such thinking was inherently autocratic—a textbook case of "rule by me" verging on totalitarianism.

Qu's interpretation became paradigmatic, representing mainstream modern scholarly views on Confucian virtue [5]. For example, Wang Boqi observed in his essay *Rule of Law and Rule of Virtue*: "In our traditional thought, the relationship between 'rule of virtue' and 'rule of law' ultimately manifests as 'rule by men' versus 'rule by law.' The two are interchangeable—advocating 'rule by men' is tantamount to advocating 'rule of virtue'" [6]. Similarly, Yang Naichang, writing in the same period, argued that "rule of rite" operated in tandem with "rule of virtue", and that both concepts, when pushed to their logical extreme, culminated in "rule by men" [7].

II. Yang Honglie: The First Proponent of the "Virtue Given Priority over Penalty" Theory

The scholar who first systematically summarized Confucian thought on the relationship between virtue and punishment as the "virtue given priority over penalty" doctrine in an academic textbook was likely Yang Honglie, a foundational figure in the discipline of the history of Chinese legal thought. In his monumental work *A History of Chinese Legal Thought*, Yang devoted an entire section in Chapter 4(The Era of Confucian Dominance) to examining ancient China's "virtue given priority over penalty" ideology. One distinctive feature of Yang's *A History of Chinese Legal Thought* is his methodology: rather than offering extensive personal commentary, he primarily compiled and categorized classical texts under labels such as "such-and-such thought". While his work meticulously collates historical discussions on "virtue given priority over penalty", Yang himself refrained from analyzing these materials or explaining why he grouped them under this framework—nor did he clarify the substantive meaning of the term. This is not to say, however, that Yang's work was a mere compilation of sources devoid of perspective. In transitional passages between quoted materials, he often inserted "interpretive ligaments"—brief but revealing commentaries that expressed his own views.

From these "interpretive ligaments", we can discern Yang's interpretation of "virtue given priority over penalty" as being grounded in two key dimensions:

Firstly, the "virtue given priority over penalty" theory is approached as a discourse on the relationship between law and virtue in ancient China. The historical materials Yang cited regarding this doctrine predominantly consisted of Confucian discussions on the importance of moral transformation and virtue education. This reveals that, in Yang's view, the essence of "virtue given priority over penalty" lay in its emphasis on virtue cultivation as primary. He interpreted it as Confucianism advocating virtue as the fundamental tool of governance, with law serving merely as a subsidiary means to realize virtue ends. Consequently, when reviewing modern scholarly works, Yang classified Liu Shipei's *Divergence between Confucianism and Legalism* as part of the "virtue given priority over penalty" discourse. However, Liu's essay actually critiqued Confucians for empty moral rhetoric while neglecting legal expertise, aiming instead to highlight the importance of judicial professionalism.

Secondly, Yang framed the "virtue given priority over penalty" doctrine through the lens of Confucian "virtue" and "rule of virtue". He explicitly stated that this idea originated with pre-Qin Confucianism, asserting: "*The principle of virtue given priority over penalty was a consistent Confucian doctrine inherited from Confucius in the Spring and Autumn period to Mencius in the Warring States era*" [8]. For Yang, "virtue given priority over penalty" was an integral part of Confucian "rule of rite", which prioritized moral-ritual education in political rule. His analysis implicitly polarized "rule of rite" and "rule of law": "rule of rite" represented the Confucian ideal, and "rule of law" epitomized Legalist thought. For instance, Yang's commentary on post-Han Dynasty applications of "virtue given priority over penalty" stated:

> Legal officials stubbornly upheld 'rule of law,' claiming that 'law alone could meet the demands of the times'. These were essentially echoes of Warring States Legalism. Yet after the great debates, even those few who later advocated 'rule of law' no longer represented authentic Legalism. Thus, Confucian 'rule of rite' or the 'virtue given priority over penalty' ultimately prevailed. [9]

In Yang Honglie's work, "rule of rite" is essentially synonymous with "rule of virtue", which from a certain perspective can also be termed "rule by men". From the perspective of governance methods, "virtue given priority over penalty" equates to so-called rule of virtue which manages society primarily through virtue transformation or virtue education, rather than ruling via legal norms. From the perspective of relationship between law and virtue, it implies a conflation of virtue and law, where the purpose of law is to realize virtue ideals, and virtue itself is seen as a higher form of law. Ultimately, the core issue with Yang's interpretation lies in his oversimplified understanding of Confucian "rule of virtue". He conflates

Confucian rule of virtue with rule of rite, and reduces the practice of rule of virtue to mere "virtue education". With these misconceptions, it becomes inevitable to conclude that "virtue given priority over penalty" blurs the distinction between law and virtue.

If Yang Honglie was the first to formally define the conceptual scope of "virtue given priority over penalty" in his textbook—identifying it as a key component of Confucian "rule of virtue"—then Qu Tongzu went further by systematically analyzing its theoretical structure and contrasting it with Legalist "rule of law". Qu's comparative framework and core arguments, as presented in his work, have since become mainstream interpretations in Chinese mainland legal historiography. His influence is so profound that it has shaped the basic structure of modern legal history textbooks, and even their methodological approach [10].

2 The Inner Logic of Modern Misinterpretations of Confucian "Virtue"

I. The Intellectual Current of Critiquing Traditional Culture

Since the New Culture Movement, a group of radical intellectuals attributed China's modern decline to inherent cultural inferiority, with Confucianism, symbolized by Confucius' thought, serving as the spiritual representation of Chinese culture. Consequently, a comprehensive critique and reexamination of Confucian culture and traditional Chinese culture emerged during this period. These radical intellectuals identified Confucius as the representative of Confucian culture, viewing his theory as the root cause that had suppressed China's spiritual development and civilizational progress for two thousand years. They believed that beneath the facade of Confucian "ritual teachings" lay cultural oppression and dehumanizing virtue constraints. Therefore, to establish a "new morality" and "new culture", it was necessary to first thoroughly criticize the "old thought" and "old culture" advocated by Confucianism. The primary target of this anti-Confucian criticism was the concept of "rite" promoted by Confucianism, which radical intellectuals consistently labeled as "ritual teachings". In 1919, Wu Yu, known for critiquing Confucianism, published his work *The Feudal Ethical Code and Its Carnivorous Logic* in *New Youth*, portraying Confucian "ritual" as spiritual shackles and the epitome of a "cannibalistic culture". Following this, radical intellectuals launched a complete denunciation of Confucian ritual thought, even demonizing what was originally a humanistic "ritual culture".

In the movement, rational critique of Confucianism did not dominate the mainstream. Instead, it primarily led to the demonization of Confucian culture. After the New Culture Movement, Confucius and Confucianism increasingly became symbols of "despotism", "feudalism", and "old culture". Under such demonized perceptions, people naturally regarded everything associated with Confucianism as despotic and based on the rule of men. Even the "virtue" advocated by Confucianism was rarely examined with fairness. Instead, it was imagined as a typical manifestation of "rule of virtue" culture rooted in the idea of the "rule by men". This created the impression that the ruling class occupied a superior position, wielding all power and possessing inherent virtue superiority, while the common people were inherently ignorant and devoid of "virtue", thus requiring enlightenment from the ruling class.

Additionally, in the 1930s and 1940s, a group of scholars who identified themselves as "New Enlighteners" and claimed to be inheritors of the New Culture Movement launched a thorough critique of Confucian culture. Among them, Chen Boda was a prominent figure. He stated, "We should heed the call of the May Fourth era to critiquing Confucianism and continue a comprehensive and systematic critique of China's old traditional thoughts and old religions" [11]. Some scholars have pointed out that these self-proclaimed new enlighteners revised Hu Shi's original proposition of critiquing Confucianism. They transformed the moderate critique of traditional culture, which was originally based on rational organization of national heritage, into a complete rejection of traditional culture, characterized by bigotry and irrationality [12].

During the evolution of modern thought from the New Culture Movement to the New Enlightenment, scholars' attitudes toward traditional culture, especially Confucian culture, gradually became more radical. Rational factors were far outweighed by voices of total denial, ultimately leading to a thorough critique and rejection of Confucian thought in modern academic circles. Moreover, the complete denial of traditional culture by new enlighteners such as Chen Boda had a profound and lasting impact on academic circles after 1949. All these factors contributed to the simplistic and stereotypical understanding and rejection of the Confucian concept of "virtue" among scholars.

II. Academic Imagination with Western Reference Points

A defining characteristic of modern scholars studying ancient Chinese intellectual history has been their use of Western concepts and frameworks to evaluate and analyze Chinese historical figures and ideas. Some have vividly likened this approach to "examining antiquities under the glow of foreign goods" [13]. For instance, Liang Qichao categorized Confucianism as "rule by men" and Legalism as "rule of law" in his works. These very concepts as opposing paradigms are Western imports. While using the West as a reference point for studying Chinese traditional thought is not inherently problematic—cultural comparison being a meaningful academic approach—there are degrees of methodological sophistication in such comparative studies. Modern scholarship on "rule of virtue" versus "rule of law" represents the most superficial form of analogical reasoning: applying Western conceptual frameworks to Chinese traditions, and simultaneously forcing Chinese traditional concepts to fit Western molds. This approach has yielded two problematic outcomes: Arbitrary westernization of certain Chinese historical ideas (e.g., misrepresenting Legalist theories on law application as equivalent to Western "rule of law" and then praising them uncritically); second, unwarranted denigration of traditional Chinese thought that differs from Western models (e.g., the wholesale rejection of Confucian "rule of virtue" under this analytical framework).

Under this Western-centric lens, scholars sought traces of "rule of law" in traditional culture, inevitably elevating Legalism—the school that discussed "law" most frequently in ancient China. For example, in *Biography of Guan Zhong*, Liang Qichao asserted: "Guan Zhong is renowned as a Legalist; all his policies were thoroughly imbued with the Legalist spirit" [14]. Although Liang's understanding of Legalism was not entirely reductionist (he did note Legalism's "belief in an all-powerful government and its rejection of the sanctity of individual character"), his reductive methodology of identifying Legalism as "rule of law" based on fragmented quotations became influential among later scholars. Consequently, misinterpreting Legalist discourse as "rule of law" gained traction in modern academia [15]. In contrast, Confucianism became a target of criticism for its perceived incompatibility with Western legal ideals. Through crude comparisons, Confucianism was accused of neglecting penal law while overemphasizing virtues such as filial piety, benevolence, righteousness. Scholars mischaracterized its essence, labeling it simplistically as "rule of virtue", then selectively quoted fragments from Confucian texts to reinforce this constructed narrative. Some scholars even contrasted Confucianism and Legalism directly, arguing that: Confucian "rule by men" was impractical and illogical, while legalist theory was rigorous and systematic step-by-step practicality. Confucianism's historical dominance was solely due to its utility for autocratic rulers. Modern China needed "rule of law", making Legalism worthy of revival [16].

The forced analogy that equated Legalist thought with Western-style "rule of law" while dismissing Confucian "rule of virtue" as "rule by men" led to elevating Legalism, while the Confucian thought, which inherently contains significant rule-of-law spirit, is abandoned and thoroughly denied. An even more severe consequence was that the Legalist "rule of law" spirit championed by scholars was in fact a doctrine of extreme monarchical supremacy that scorned the value of the individual. Legalism advocates sacrificing individual freedom and dignity for the sake of "enriching the country" and "strengthening the military". As noted by Zhang Taiyan, "Legalism can make a state orderly, but it cannot make it humane. It sees the state, not the people; the collective, not the individual" [17]. Modern scholars' preference for state-centric Legalism reflected the nationalist fervor of the early twentieth century, which prioritized "state over individual", a mindset that the choice of Legalism, in turn, further promoted and amplified. In contrast, Confucianism, centered on "faithfulness and reciprocity" and "harmonious balance", emphasizing human relationships and community welfare, fundamentally emphasizes the maintenance of human relations and communities. It regards the state or the monarch as a means to protect the people, rather than an end for "prosperity and strength", and was thus discarded by the academic circles of that time like worn-out shoes. The powerful state that the modern radical trend of thought hoped to create was precisely of the Legalist type. After Confucianism was thoroughly criticized, what followed was the devastating blow to society by the radical political trend of thought. The human relations communities and the political structure of "limited state with a expansive, robust civil society" that Confucianism highly valued were completely destroyed after 1949. All of this is closely related to the academic trend of "valuing Legalism over Confucianism" since modern times.

Moreover, the "virtue" advocated by Confucianism and the "power" advocated by Legalism actually correspond to each other, both being requirements for political legitimacy. The difference lies in that Confucianism holds that the foundation of political rule lies not in the possession of state violence but in the implementation of virtuous policies that win the hearts of the people. In Confucian view, violence can be used to seize power but not to govern or maintain it. However, Legalism is different. Legalism believes in the rule of strength represented by "potential" and "power". Those with great "potential" hold the world. Not only is seizing power dependent on violence, but maintaining power also requires violence. Modern scholars regard Confucian "rule of virtue" as merely a form of "rule by men" thought and overlook the significance of political legitimacy it contains. This is not unrelated to the "winner-takes-all" values that have flourished since modern times. People who blindly believe in "violence" naturally fail to see the great significance contained in the "virtue" advocated by Confucianism. Therefore, they can only regard the "rule of virtue" theory in Confucian thought as "persuasion".

3 The Insufficiency of Summarizing Traditional Virtue-Punishment Relations with "Virtue Given Priority over Penalty"

I. The Layers of the "Virtue Given Priority over Penalty" Theory

The theoretical frameworks established by Yang Honglie and Qu Tongzu have profoundly influenced modern legal historians' research on traditional Chinese thought regarding the relationship between virtue and punishment. For nearly a century, scholars have generally situated this relationship within the broader discourse on law and virtue or even more narrowly, as a debate between virtue education and penal sanctions. A closer examination of academic discussions on the "Virtue Given Priority over Penalty" theory reveals two distinct levels of interpretation: First, the "Virtue Education as Primary" View. This interpretation understands "virtue given priority over penalty" as a debate over the relative importance of virtue education versus penal sanctions. Proponents argue that the doctrine's essence lies in that virtue education plays a more constructive role in governance than punishment. Scholars frequently cite Confucius' famous dictum: "If the people are ruled by injunctions and restricted by penalty, they may try to evade the punishment without developing the sense of shame, If they are guided by morality and regulated by the rules of propriety, they will have the sense of shame and become disciplined". This illustrates Confucian emphasis on the transformative power of rite and virtue, positing that cultivating virtue among the people naturally guides them toward goodness.

Second, the "Virtuous Governance as Primary" View. It considers virtue given priority over penalty" as an extension of Confucian "rule of virtue" ideals. Confucius's saying: "He who exercises government by means of his virtue may be compared to the North Polar Star, which keeps its place while all the stars turn toward it", is frequently cited to demonstrate his support of "rule of virtue". This view treats the doctrine as a political philosophy advocating virtuous governance, where the ruler prioritizes the welfare of the people. Yang Hegao, for instance, incorporates Confucian principles of respecting popular will and people-centered governance into the core of "virtue given priority over penalty" [18]. Long Daxuan further elaborates that the doctrine, broadly construed, constitutes a statecraft strategy: it demands virtuous politics, economically prioritizes enriching and nurturing the populace, and culturally implements virtue cultivation to foster an innate aversion to crime. Scholar Geng Yunqing from Taiwan offers a unique perspective, likening Confucian "virtue given priority over penalty" thought to Western natural law theory. He argues that Western natural law, despite its evolution, remains bound by religious and ethical paradigms, wherein concepts of justice and goodness align with what ancient Chinese thinkers termed virtue education. Thus, he proposes a comparative analysis between the two traditions [19].

There are also scholars who argue that whether it is the theory of "Virtue Education as Primary" or "Virtuous Governance as Primary", the essence of both lies in the belief that the relationship between virtue and punishment summarized in the concept of "virtue given priority over penalty" is, in substance, the relationship between virtue and law. For instance, Fan Zhongxin's research suggests that in ancient China, the Confucian and Legalist schools' debate over the relationship between virtue and punishment showed no divergence in terms of the ideals of political order or the normative principles of law. The crux of the debate lay instead in the means and methods of achieving such political order, whether to emphasize punishment or virtue [20]. Similarly, scholar Wang Boqi from Taiwan (China) contends that the Confucian and Legalist schools shared no differences in the ultimate goals of moral principles, but rather diverged in their approaches and methods for realizing the same objectives [21].

II. Shortcomings of "Virtue Given Priority over Penalty"

First, the so-called virtue given priority over penalty theory fails to accurately grasp the essence of the concept of "virtue", leading to a narrow research perspective. Scholars generally hold two main views on this doctrine: (1) virtue serves as the primary governance tool, with law playing a secondary role, and (2) law is merely an instrument for achieving virtuous objectives. When examining "virtue given priority over penalty" within the framework of the relationship between law and virtue, it is easy to conclude that ancient society conflated law with virtue, creating the impression that traditional society did not value law. In reality, the ancient concept of "virtue" was not simply morality but encompassed deeper meanings. Some scholars have pointed out that "virtue" in ancient times actually represented a mode of governance opposed to "rule of punishment".

Second, existing interpretations of "virtue given priority over penalty" often conflate "virtue" with "rite". In previous studies, some scholars have summarized traditional Chinese thought on the relationship between virtue and punishment using terms like "the unity of rite and punishment" or "rite given priority over penalty", neglecting the unique value and connotations of the ancient concept of "virtue". Regarding the distinction between "virtue" and "rite", "virtue" leans more toward the spiritual dimension, while "rite" more pertains to external norms. As "virtue" and "rite" evolved and diverged, "virtue" and "conduct" also gradually separated. The element of "conduct" inherent in "virtue" diminished over time, becoming externalized and absorbed into "rite", while "virtue" turned inward, becoming a matter of spiritual values and ethical principles.

Third, in terms of research on the model of "rule of virtue", current scholarship remains largely confined to exploring the legitimizing function of virtue and its role in governing the state. Existing studies have so far failed to adequately respond to the following critiques of "rule of virtue": (1) traditional politics, by defining legitimacy through "virtue", could not escape the dilemmas of rule of virtue and the lack of institutional constraints on power; and (2) the traditional rule of virtue model struggles to withstand the challenges posed by modern rule of law. These issues stem primarily from insufficient research on the role of virtue education in shaping the social order of traditional China. Traditional society relied on Confucian virtue and rite indoctrination to cultivate shared values and social cohesion among the populace. The significance of rule of virtue lay in its bottom-up approach, mobilizing society's capacity for self-governance.

Bibliography

1. Liaoyuan, C. (2011). "Native goods" illuminated by "foreign imports": Approaches and divergent views on modern Chinese critiques of legalist "rule of law" thought. *Modern Law Science.*
2. Liang Qichao's classification of pre-Qin political trends of thought, particularly the opposition between rule of virtue and rule of law, was tremendously influential at the time. Numerous subsequent writings were clearly influenced by Liang's framework. For instance, the following article is essentially a restatement of Liang's thesis: Naichang, Y. (1934). The doctrine of rule of rite and the doctrine of rule of law. *New Trend, 93.*
3. Zhenxian, W. (1925). *The science of law in Ancient China* (p. 49). The Commercial Press.
4. Tongzu, Q. (1989). *Law and society in traditional China* (Vol. 29, p. 232). "Republican Series" First Collection. Shanghai Bookstore Publishing House.
5. There are also exceptions. For instance, some scholars in their works categorized pre-Qin political thought into four types: the doctrine of rule of virtue, the doctrine of rule of law, the doctrine of non-governance, and the doctrine of rule by men. This view actually represents a misunderstanding of rule by men. If we follow Qu Tongzu's explanation of rule of virtue, then rule of virtue is indeed a form of rule by men. Shaozhe, L. (1934). A brief account of Confucian doctrine of rule of virtue and doctrine of rule of rite. *Youth and War, 4*(10).
6. Boqi, W. (1999). *Rule of law and rule of virtue, collected legal works of Wang Boqi* (p. 104). Sanmin Book Company.
7. Naichang, Y. (1934). The doctrine of rule of rite and the doctrine of rule of law. *New Trend, 93.*
8. Honglie, Y. (1937). *History of Chinese legal thought* (Vol. 2, p. 12). The Commercial Press.
9. Honglie, Y. (1937). *History of Chinese legal thought* (Vol. 2, p. 35). The Commercial Press.
10. From the perspective of textbook compilation style and structural framework, mainland legal history or intellectual history textbooks follow the

model of Yang Honglie, essentially presenting as chronological histories or spectrums of thinkers. However, issues such as "the Confucianization of Law" and "the Incorporation of Rite into Law" proposed by Qu Tongzu in his work are unavoidable in any textbook.

11. Boda, C. (1936). Philosophical national defense mobilization: A self-criticism by new philosophers and a proposal for the new enlightenment movement. *Reading Life, 4*(9).
12. Kefeng, M. (2011). Analysis of "pounding the Confucian shop" versus "overthrowing the Confucian shop". *Journal of Renmin University of China, 2.*
13. Liaoyuan,C. (2011). Native goods illuminated by foreign imports: Approaches and divergent views on modern Chinese critiques of legalist 'rule of law' thought. *Modern Law Science.*
14. Qichao, L. (1985). Biography of Guan Zhong. In Z. Pinxing (ed.), *The complete works of Liang Qichao* (Vol. 6, p. 1858). Beijing Publishing House.
15. For example, the Republican-era scholar Sun Bide, in his article *The Spirit of the Rule of Law in Our Country*, categorized Daoism as advocating non-governance (wu zhi), Mohism as advocating divine governance (tian zhi), and argued that Confucianism, resembling educators, advocated rule of man (ren zhi) and emphasized transformative education. He posited that only Legalist thought possessed the most significant elements of rule of law, employing interventionism and representing practical statesmanship. Bide, S. (1944). The spirit of the rule of law in our country. *Aurora Journal of Law and Economics, 1*(2–3).
16. Ruxuan, C., "Rule by men" and "Rule of law". *The Times Review, 88.*
17. Taiyan, T. (2003). *Discourses on national heritage* (p. 115). Shanghai Ancient Books Publishing House.
18. Hegao, Y. (1986). *A preliminary study on the formation of the Confucian theory of "virtue given priority over penalty", studies on Confucius' legal thought (collection of essays)* (p. 203). Shandong People's Publishing House.
19. Yunqing, G. (1982). *Pre-Qin legal thought and natural law* (p. 55). The Commercial Press of Taiwan.
20. Zhongxin, F. (1991). *The true meaning of the debate on the relative importance of virtue and punishment in Ancient China. Journal of Comparative Law, 1.*
21. Boqi, W. (1956). Modern legal thought and Chinese indigenous culture, judicial administration (p. 12). Department of Taiwan, p. 12.

CHAPTER 5

A Sino-Western Comparison of the Relationship Between Virtue and Law

1 Chinese "Virtue" vs. Western Law and Rule of Law

I. Conceptual Distinctions Between "Virtue" and "Law"

The Chinese concept of "virtue" in ancient times was a multi-layered and richly connotative idea, carrying different meanings in various contexts. In this paper, we focus specifically on the Confucian conception of "virtue", particularly its significance and scope within the modern academic framework of "virtue given priority over penalty". From our earlier analysis, we find that pre-Qin Confucian "virtue" had dual dimensions—political and personal. In terms of the political dimension, it encompasses three distinct levels of meaning: virtuous governance, rule of virtue, and virtue education. Virtuous governance refers to political virtue, implying that rule must possess legitimacy. Confucians elucidate the connotations and scope of political virtue through two aspects: the ideal paradigm of kingly way politics and the rectification of names. The kingly way politics serves as an ideal model, providing a critical standard for real-world politics. The rectification of names is the primary means to uphold political virtue, as Confucians use it to clarify the rights and obligations between the ruler and subjects, ensuring that each fulfills their respective roles and adheres to their virtue duties. Rule of virtue and virtue education are interrelated

D. Li, *Conceptual History of Morality and Penalty in China*, Key Concepts in Chinese Thought and Culture,
https://doi.org/10.1007/978-981-95-9059-9_5

as goals and means. Regarding the governance model, the Confucian approach to social governance can be termed rule of virtue, while virtue education serves as the primary method to achieve this end. In the personal dimension, "virtue" refers to the moral qualities that individuals should possess. In Confucian thought, virtue is rooted in the human heart and nature, making it accessible to all individuals regardless of social status. Officials are expected to uphold official virtue, while common people should possess civic virtue. Confucianism first emphasizes the establishment of official virtue, demanding that rulers practice virtuous governance and rule by virtue. Subsequently, it stresses the importance of cultivating civic virtue among the people, hoping that through education, individuals can become self-reliant and self-cultivated. Ultimately, this leads to the ruler's effortless governance, avoiding frequent interference by rulers in the normal order of civilian life through policies and punishments.

The differences between ancient and modern conceptions of "law" are even more complex. Traditional Chinese "law" and Western "law" differ fundamentally, not merely as apples from different orchards, but as bananas and oranges, to borrow Zhu Suli's metaphor [1]. Yan Fu, while translating Montesquieu's *The Spirit of the Laws*, recognized this divergence, noting: "The Western term 'law' corresponds variably in Chinese to 'rite', 'principle', 'statute', and 'institution'. Western 'law' actually encompasses what Chinese tradition calls 'rite and code'" [2]. Though Yan Fu addressed Sino-Western differences, China's legal modernization since the late Qing reforms has largely adopted Western legal traditions. Thus, the historical shift in China's concept of "law" mirrors the East–West contrast he identified. Expanding on Yan Fu's insight, we can identify three key divergences between ancient and modern "law": Firstly, there are differences in connotative scope. The modern concept of "law" encompasses both positive law and natural law. In contrast, the ancient Chinese concept of "law" primarily referred to the normative statutes promulgated by the state, manifesting in various specific legal forms of ancient society, such as laws, edicts, regulations, formulas, precedents, or codes. The connotations of natural law within the modern concept of "law" were, in ancient times, more commonly embodied in the concepts of reason or rite [3]. Secondly, there are differences in forms of expression. Past scholarship has often interpreted the forms of expression of ancient "law" from the perspective of the modern concept of "law" to highlight differences between ancient and modern times. For instance, it has been argued that ancient law was primarily codified, reflecting characteristics of "prioritizing punishment, with no distinction between criminal and civil law". However, such interpretations frequently overlook the differences in the forms of expression between ancient and modern concepts of "law". In its modern sense, the concept of "law" in ancient times encompassed not only statutory laws and regulations as codified by the state but also rite as the "foundation" of the ancient legal system, as well as a vast array of community rules and family regulations that possessed legal qualities. Thirdly, there are differences in methods of regulation. The primary means by which ancient law regulated social relations were rewards and punishments. However, a review of historical statutes and edicts reveals that the regulation of social relations by law placed greater emphasis on punishment. Consequently, a sole examination of "law" in ancient society could easily lead to the conclusion that the Chinese legal system was "primarily criminal" in nature.

Regarding the relationship between virtue and law, if we examine it from the perspective of the ancient concept of "law", then in traditional society, the relationship between virtue and law often manifested as one of opposition and complementarity between "virtue" and "punishment". As previously discussed, virtue and punishment frequently appeared as paired antithetical concepts, particularly in *Zuo Zhuan*, where they were juxtaposed to emphasize their equally indispensable roles in governance. For instance, *Zuo Zhuan* defines their relationship thus: "To quell rebellion is the function of punishment; to pacify submission is the function of virtue" [4]. "Virtue restrains wickedness; punishment suppresses disorder. Where neither virtue nor punishment is established, wickedness and disorder will arise together" [5]. In this framework, virtue and punishment stand in opposition: Virtue operates through methods of "appeasement", "conciliation", and "leniency"—employing benevolent means to pacify the people. Punishment, by contrast, employs methods of "subjugation", "suppression", and "deterrence"—relying on coercive force to crush rebellion. It was precisely through the Spring and Autumn period thinkers' reflections on the distinct political logics of virtue and punishment that later generations developed the philosophy of "emphasizing both virtue and punishment" or "balancing leniency and severity". This duality even influenced the strategic principle of "alternating civil and martial governance", which traces its roots to the hegemonic strategies of the Spring and Autumn era that juxtaposed virtue and punishment. Through the intellectual debates between Confucians and Legalists during the pre-Qin period, virtue and punishment gradually evolved into two opposing models of governance: Confucian virtue-based governance and Legalist punishment-centric rule.

It should be noted that the Confucian concept of "virtue" in ancient China carried different connotations depending on context. However, when juxtaposed with "punishment", "virtue" primarily referred to "rule of virtue" as a mode of social administration that stood in opposition to the Legalist "rule of punishment". Thus, the "virtue-punishment" duality in the classical principle of "virtue given priority over penalty" does not simply denote an opposition between "morality versus penalties", or "leniency versus severity" as governance techniques. Rather, it represents a hierarchical relationship between two governance paradigms: the Confucian rule of virtue served as the dominant framework, while selectively incorporating practical institutional measures from Legalist rule of punishment approaches. Examining traditional Chinese governance through this lens reveals that "virtue" and "punishment" maintained an ontological hierarchy of "essence-function": Confucian rule of virtue shaped the core values, spirit, and fundamental models of China's political-legal tradition and legalist punitive methods were pragmatically adopted as instrumental means for specific administrative needs.

Contemporary scholarship commonly characterizes the relationship between Confucianism and Legalism in the political framework of imperial China as "Taking Legalism in the name of Confucianism". This formulation has been interpreted in two predominant ways: the state ostensibly embodied Confucian benevolent governance, while its actual operations followed Legalist authoritarian principles. Or, Confucianism shaped societal ethics, whereas Legalism constituted the institutional ethos [6]. However, through our examination of the institutional implementation of the Confucian principle "Virtue given priority over penalty", we propose a necessary reinterpretation. The core institutional spirit and fundamental governance framework of traditional China were fundamentally molded by Confucian's rule of virtue. Virtue served as the ultimate criterion for political legitimacy and institutional rationality. While, the externalization of virtue through ritual norms directly constituted: the foundational spirit of traditional Chinese law and the political architecture of imperial governance.

II. Chinese "Virtue" vs. Western Law and Rule of Law

When modern scholars introduced the Western concept of "rule of law" into China, they misinterpreted its true meaning by translating it as "*fazhi*". In reality, the Western notion of "rule of law" encompasses both positive law and natural law, whereas the Chinese term "*fa*" typically refers only to state law—that is, coercive norms. Consequently, since modern times, "*fazhi*" in the Chinese context has come to mean merely "rule of law", or even "rule by coercion", stripping away the Western legal concept's connotations of "divine order" and "natural law". Under the lens of Western comparison, scholars sought traces of "rule of law" in traditional Chinese thought, leading them to elevate Legalism, the school that discussed "law" most extensively in ancient China. For example, Liang Qichao, in *Biography of Guan Zhong*, argued: "Whether constitutional or autocratic, any state calling itself a polity must rely on the spirit of the rule of law to sustain itself. This is precisely the case. Guan Zhong, as a Legalist, infused all his policies with this spirit" [7]. Liang's view is representative of the era, essentially reducing the rule of law to a simplistic "rule by law". Some scholars even claim that Legalism proposed a "minimalist version of the rule of law", arguing that the only difference between Legalist governance and modern Western formalist rule of law lies in whether the legislator is a monarch or the people. They suggest that, with a shift in historical context, the concepts of "monarch" and "people" could be logically transposed in legal methodology, thus offering a universalist pathway for modernizing Legalist thought [8]. However, this "minimalist conception of rule of law" is a purely logical construct divorced from historical practice and social values. It not only fails to explain why Legalism led to the extreme authoritarianism of the tyrannical Qin Dynasty but also proves incapable of achieving good governance, thereby trapping itself in theoretical contradictions. Once scholars classify Legalism as formalist rule of law, they struggle to reconcile why such formalism could produce totalitarian regimes like the Qin or Nazi Germany, leading them to question the very validity of formalist rule of law and plunging into self-contradiction [9].

Modern scholarship's oversimplified understanding of the rule of law has not only misrepresented it but also distorted Confucian "rule of virtue". For instance, Wang Zhenxian, a jurist of the Republican era, further promoted this binary in *Ancient Chinese Jurisprudence*. He enthusiastically endorsed Legalist thought as embodying "rule of law", even listing figures like Zhuge Liang and Fu Jian as advocates. The inevitable corollary was his critique of Confucian "rule by men" and "rule of virtue". Wang attributed China's perceived underdevelopment of legal institutions solely to the "exclusive worship of Confucianism", condemning not only Confucian governance theories but also Han Dynasty legal commentaries for "merely engaging in literal interpretations, utterly divorced from the original spirit of the Warring States Legalists" [10]. These misunderstandings of Confucian "rule of virtue" stem from scholars applying a narrow, rigid concept of "rule of law" to traditional legal thought. Under such a framework, the intrinsic connection between Confucian "virtue" and modern rule of law inevitably remains obscured.

First, Confucian "virtue" is a requirement for the legitimacy of state power. The fundamental difference between "virtue" and "punishment" lies in the fact that "virtue" imposes demands on the legitimacy of ruling power. Confucian political thought compels people to reflect on the issue of the political legitimacy of power—what kind of person is worthy of wielding power, and how power should be exercised legitimately. These questions find answers within the Confucian concept of "virtue". In contrast, the Legalist approach of "rule of punishment" does no such thing. It fundamentally denies the significance of the legitimacy of power, asserting that in politics, power is a symbol of strength. And those who possess strength hold power, and "power" is inseparable from "strength". Viewing the Confucian concept of "virtue" from the perspective of legitimacy reveals that it not only does not conflict with modern rule of law but also shares an intrinsic connection with it, even aiding our reflection on contemporary notions of the rule of law. In contemporary discourse, there are two diametrically opposed understandings of the essence of the rule of law. Among them, the "formalist" theory of the rule of law defines it solely based on the formal requirements of law, severing the intrinsic connection between the rule of law and morality. In terms of value orientation, it leans toward the realization of formal justice, and in the application of law, it adheres to the positivist stance, emphasizing interpretation to ensure the full implementation of law. From the perspective of attitudes toward law, the Qin Dynasty's "rule of punishment" closely resembles the "formalist" theory of the rule of law—for instance, in its demands for the publicity, universality, and stability of law. This sufficiently demonstrates that defining the rule of law solely from a formalist perspective is inadequate. The formalist theory of the rule of law, in real political practice, is fundamentally insufficient to distinguish between autocratic rule of law and democratic rule of law. At its extreme, it becomes an instrumentalist theory of the rule of law. In contrast, the Confucian concept of "virtue" contemplates the legitimacy of politics, reflecting on the moral qualities that politics ought to possess from a substantive perspective. Precisely for this reason, it can serve as a supplement to the "instrumentalism" theory of the rule of law. Confucian "rule of virtue" helps us re-examine the significance of "virtue" for politics and the rule of law, establishing an intrinsic connection between law and morality. The legitimacy of law does not ultimately derive from state authority but rather from the inherent rationality and legitimacy of law itself.

Second, Confucian "rule of virtue" stands in direct opposition to Legalist "rule of punishment". Following the Legalist path of "rule of punishment" ultimately leads to tyranny, subjugating all aspects of society under the domination of punishment. This not only subjects the people to the terror of harsh penalties but also disrupts the natural development of society. State political order becomes monopolized by punishment, leaving no society outside the state and no social authority beyond the monarch's power that governs the people's daily lives. Ultimately, this erodes the mechanisms and capacity for self-governance in society as a whole. Confucian "rule of virtue" does not disregard law or punishment; rather, the "rite" proposed by pre-Qin Confucianism essentially represent the standardization and institutionalization of social customs, functioning not only as law but also holding higher efficacy than law. The fundamental distinction between "rule of virtue" and "rule of punishment" lies in the Confucian insistence that, in the process of social governance, greater emphasis should be placed on the significance of "virtue education". In its most immediate sense, virtue education does not inflict physical harm, and its emphasis aims to reduce cruel punishments. This reflects Confucian efforts to humanize the legal system in ancient society, adding a civilized dimension to China's otherwise severe legal history. On a deeper level, Confucianism sought to cultivate scholar-gentlemen through virtue education. These gentlemen, deeply influenced by Confucian cultural beliefs, were dispersed among the populace, not only strengthening social cohesion and serving as crucial bridges between officials and the people but also fostering a robust self-governance mechanism among the common people. In summary, compared to the Legalist "rule of punishment", "rule of virtue" strives to cultivate society's self-governance mechanisms, emphasizing rite and music, and respect for teachers and elders, ultimately enabling the full development of civil society and the formation of social authority independent of monarchical power. From the perspective of governance models, Confucian "rule of virtue" not only does not conflict with modern democratic politics but can also contribute to the cultivation of high-quality citizens and the formation of effective social self-governance mechanisms in modern democracies.

To argue that "rule of virtue" can serve as a supplement to democratic rule of law is not to claim that ancient China, which practiced "rule of virtue", was not a rule by men. The ancient Chinese political system, characterized by imperial autocracy, was undoubtedly a typical example of rule of man. However, its emergence stemmed from diverse causes and cannot be simplistically attributed to "rule of virtue" or the principle of "virtue given priority over penalty". At the same time, we must not equate "rule of virtue" with rule by men simply because it emerged within a political framework of rule by men, thereby dismissing it entirely and overlooking its profound significance.

2 The Moral Dilemma in the Construction of Rule of Law in Transitional China

The rule of law has become one of the most discussed topics in China today, yet it is also one of the most perplexing issues. Looking back at the four decades of legal development since the reform and opening-up, we find that the state has primarily focused on constructing a legal system and judicial framework while neglecting the virtue foundation and social environment necessary for the rule of law. In reflecting on the state-led legislative approach to legal construction, scholars have come to recognize the inherent limitations of relying solely on statutory laws to meet the demands of social order [11]. The legal development centered on state legislation reflects a tendency toward constructivist rule of law. Constructivist rule of law inevitably bears the characteristics of state-dominated planning and design, manifesting in governance as an overreliance on legislation while disregarding the positive role of local knowledge, such as virtue and customs in social governance [12]. More importantly, state legislation cannot fully replace society's inherent capacity to generate order, nor can it provide the necessary virtue foundation and value consensus for establishing a society governed by law.

Some scholars describe the social issues China faces during its transitional period as the "transition trap". One of the symptoms of this "transition trap" is the increasing visibility of social fragmentation and social decay [13]. Antagonism between different social strata has intensified, making it difficult to establish a societal consensus and widening the divide between classes. The lack of shared values has left society without a basic ethical foundation, leading to widespread anomie and moral decline, a phenomenon also referred to as "social decay". It can be said that the greatest challenge China faces in its current transitional phase is the ethical vacuum and behavioral anomie resulting from this absence of consensus. In the realm of the rule of law, this social issue manifests as a persistent virtue deficit in China's legal construction. The virtue dilemma in China's "rule of law" development during the transitional period is primarily reflected in the following three aspects: First, the state-led "rule of virtue" is a top-down moral campaign, similar in nature to the rational constructivism that dominates China's "rule of law" approach. The current state-promoted "rule of virtue" primarily takes the form of moral propaganda, disseminating officially endorsed values and ethical standards (e.g., the "Eight Honors and Eight Shames" or Socialist Core Values) through a centralized publicity apparatus. In this campaign, the establishment and diffusion of certain moral norms are inseparable from the forceful push of political power. Using political power to enforce moral standards effectively rigidifies and universalizes a particular ethical framework, which is functionally akin to legalizing morality. Some scholars argue that such a "rule of virtue" not only undermines the formal rationality and relative autonomy of law but also, paradoxically, stifles virtue progress while promoting virtue, ultimately breeding widespread hypocrisy [14]. Morality, by its very nature, should be free and pluralistic, yet state-driven moral campaigns impose fixed standards, leaving no room for organic evolution. Moral order is fundamentally an endogenous order, best cultivated organically within civil society through the subtle guidance of local gentry or intellectuals, gradually shaping societal ethical consensus. The proper role of the modern state should be limited to fostering an institutional and social environment conducive to nurturing such morally exemplary groups, rather than directly imposing moral norms.

Second, modern rule of law, constructed primarily through state rationalist legislation, has led to disconnect between legal institutions and social reality. This disjunction manifests most acutely in the lack of value consensus, where the values promoted by law clash with traditional societal ethics, leaving the public alienated from legal norms. The foundational values of modern rule of law are rooted in individualism, emphasizing personal rights and freedoms, which fundamentally conflicts with traditional Chinese communitarian and collectivist values prioritizing communal interests. State attempts to mediate this conflict through legislation often prove ineffective. For instance, *the Law on the Protection of the Rights of the Elderly* sought to codify filial piety (e.g., mandating adult children to "visit home often"), blending traditional ethics with modern legal norms. Such provisions are not only unenforceable but also highlight the inherent value conflicts in legislating morality. Legal consensus cannot be imposed through state legislation alone; it requires gradual moral transformation within society itself, fostering shared values that ultimately align with the spirit of the rule of law.

Third, the foundation of rule of law construction dominated by legal constructionism lies in national legislation and the legal system primarily formed by it. Over the past three decades of legal development, China's legal system has mainly centered on national legislation. One characteristic of such a state-led legal system is the lack of social norms, as customary practices and moral standards, key components of social norms, are rarely incorporated into the legal framework. A legal system devoid of social norms struggles to integrate societal ethics and mainstream values, internalizing them as a dimension of the rule of law. A mature rule-of-law society is not only governed by state-enacted legal norms but also operates as an open system capable of assimilating moral standards, social values, and customs into its framework. This fosters a constructive interaction between state laws and social norms, a dynamic that embodies legal pluralism. As noted, "One consequence of legal pluralism is the increased opportunity for participation within legal procedures" [15]. In an effective interaction mechanism between law and morality, morality serves as the value premise and foundation of law, providing essential criteria for judging its righteousness. At the same time, the law preserves autonomy for morality, neither requiring legal enforcement of moral practices nor relying on legislation to drive moral progress.

To address the issue of moral absence in China's current development of the rule of law, it is necessary to draw on the experience of rule of virtue in traditional Confucian political philosophy. When presiding over the 37th collective study of the Political Bureau of the CPC Central Committee, Comrade Xi Jinping pointed out that it is essential to strengthen the supporting role of morality for the rule of law. To uphold the combination of governing the country according to law and governing the country with virtue, it is necessary to emphasize the role of morality in moral education, raise the level of civilization across society, and create a favorable cultural environment for comprehensively governing the country according to law [15]. While emphasizing the combination of governing the country according to law and governing the country with virtue, it should be noted that rule of virtue is not actually a governance model opposed to or parallel to the rule of law. In the political philosophy system of ancient Confucianism, what was opposed to "rule of virtue" was the "rule of punishment" of the Legalists. In the process of social governance, Confucian rule of virtue first emphasizes the legitimacy of rulers and their governance mechanisms, demanding that politics and corresponding legal systems should possess virtue. Secondly, it requires that the literati and officials enhance the virtue standards of the people through virtue education to cultivate social self-governance capabilities [16]. Therefore, the rule of virtue emphasized by Confucianism is not actually opposed to the rule of law and can serve as an important foundation and component of modern rule of law.

3 Co-governance of Virtue and Law: The Potential Value of Confucianism in Contemporary Chinese Governance

In recent years, academic discussions on "Mainland Neo-Confucianism" have revolved around debates between "inner-mind Confucianism" and "political Confucianism". Political Confucianism argues that Confucianism is primarily a philosophy of institutional reform and legislation rather than merely a philosophy of self-cultivation and virtue attainment. Thus, it contends that Confucianism's potential contribution during China's transition period should lie in proposing a new Confucian political framework rather than limiting it to introspective virtue philosophy [17]. However, the Confucian political structures designed by political Confucianism for China's transformation have faced criticism from political science and legal scholars. Given the highly complex and short-term nature of modern societal interests, political Confucianism not only lacks practical applicability but also risks damaging Confucianism's credibility if it is ideologized [18]. Revisiting the original essence of Confucian "rule of virtue" can help us better understand its potential contributions to contemporary China. Confucian moral philosophy, which emphasizes self-cultivation and ethical refinement, is not merely about personal ethics but carries profound political significance—cultivating civic virtue and grass-roots autonomy through the exemplary conduct of scholar-gentlemen. The legal and political institutions designed by traditional Confucianism were also intended to refine human nature within a framework of rite, music, punishment, and governance, thereby regulating human conduct. Therefore, Confucian rule of virtue actually bridges inner-mind Confucianism and political Confucianism. To discuss Confucian virtue without considering its political dimensions would strip it of its deeper role in moral transformation and social customs.

A feasible path for Confucianism to contribute to modern governance lies in enriching the current rule of law with a moral dimension—what is termed the "integration of rule of virtue and rule of law". In today's legal construction, attention must be paid to transforming and innovating governance methods to invigorate social organizations. A key challenge is balancing state-society relations to achieve positive interaction between government governance, social self-regulation, and resident autonomy. Addressing contemporary governance dilemmas requires drawing lessons from both Chinese and Western historical and modern governance experiences to refine governance methods and energize social organizations. Reflecting on Confucian conceptions of "virtue" and its governance logic, we find an emphasis on virtue and rite education as crucial to social governance. Confucian efforts to refine customs and rectify minds through moral influence actually enhanced the self-governing capacity of civil society. In the short term, Confucian virtue governance helped ease tensions between rulers and the people, as well as officials and citizens. In the long term, Confucian "rule of virtue" relied on local gentry who embodied Confucian values, setting examples and fostering shared values and consensus, thereby leading rural communities to develop self-governing structures and mechanisms. These measures all contributed to the healthy development of grassroots autonomy. Confucian virtue-centered governance does not conflict with modern rule of law; rather, Confucian virtue education can complement legal governance. More importantly, the social consensus urgently needed in China today cannot be formed solely through a constructivist rule of law dominated by state legislation. The formation of social consensus requires a solid moral foundation and institutional environment, necessitating the integration of both social and moral dimensions in the process of legal construction.

The contribution Confucianism can make in contemporary society lies primarily in the reinterpretation and revitalization of its philosophy of "rule of virtue". The idea of reconstructing so-called Confucian institutions by detaching from modern politics is not only unrealistic but also represents a top-down, rationally constructed institutional system—one that inherently contradicts Confucianism's bottom-up "rule of virtue" order. Therefore, the greatest contribution Confucianism can offer during China's political and social transformation is to provide a moral dimension to the ongoing building of the rule of law, thereby forming a governance system characterized by the integrated rule of virtue and law. First, Confucian "rule of virtue" bridges the divide between "inner-mind Confucianism" and "political Confucianism". While the core Confucian ideal indeed centers on self-cultivation and virtue attainment, it is crucial to note that the "self" here refers primarily to rulers, and the "virtue" in question pertains to the political virtues rulers ought to possess. Second, Confucian discourse on moral self-cultivation was never solely about personal ethics; its fundamental purpose was to elevate the virtue of the people through moral transformation and custom-shaping, thereby fostering a self-governing society. As Liang Qichao observed regarding Confucian "rule of virtue": "Confucianism firmly believed that without sound citizens, there could be no sound governance. Hence, its approach to governance focused solely on nurturing political morality, capability, and habits among the majority" [19]. The Confucian emphasis on rite and music aimed to cultivate the basic moral qualities of the people. With virtuous citizens, there would be no need for sagely rulers to steer or lead, nor for intrusive interference in people's lives—no threats of punishment or political coercion would be necessary, as a just political order would emerge naturally. Finally, Confucian "virtue" is not limited to the moral character of rulers and subjects alone. It also concerns institutional virtue, demanding that institutional design align with human nature rather than distort it. From a Confucian perspective, any institutional design detached from human sentiments, nature, and social experience is inherently flawed—this applies not only to blindly copying Western systems but also to idealized Confucian governance models conceived through pure rational construction. Whether an institution possesses virtue depends entirely on its capacity to allow human nature to flourish freely.

Bibliography

1. Li, S. (1998). The story of law. *Reading, 7.*
2. Fu, Y. (1981). *The spirit of the laws by Montesquieu* (pp. 3, 7). The Commercial Press.
3. Xianyi, Z., & Xiaohong, M. (2003). *The structure and basic concepts of traditional Chinese law: On the relationship between Ancient rite and law. Social Sciences in China, 5.*
4. *Zuo Zhuan: The twelfth year of Duke Xuan.*
5. *Zuo Zhuan: The seventeen year of Duke Cheng.*
6. Xiaobo, W. (2015, November 30). Overt Confucianism and covert legalism" as the mainstream of Chinese culture. *Guangming Daily.*
7. Qichao, L. (1985). Biography of Guan Zhong. In Z. Pinxing (Ed.), *The complete works of Liang Qichao* (Vol. 6, p. 1858). Beijing Publishing House.
8. Renbo, W. (2003). A minimalist conception of the rule of law: A modern interpretation of Chinese legalist thought. *Legal Forum, 1.*
9. Daohui, G. (2005). *The essence of iurisprudence* (pp. 258–259). Hunan People's Publishing House; Hongjun, G. (2002). *Rule of law: Ideas and institutions* (p. 185). China University of Political Science and Law Press.
10. Zhenxian, W. (1925). *The science of law in Ancient China* (p. 49). The Commercial Press.
11. Zheng, P. (2016). The social dimension of the rule of law order. *Science of Law, 1.*
12. Changshan, M. (2016). *The errors and ways out of state constructivist rule of law. Law Review, 4*
13. Research Group on Social Development, Department of Sociology, Tsinghua University. (2012). "Middle-income trap" or "transition trap"? *Open Times, 3.*
14. Li, S. (2002). An analysis of the legitimacy of rule of virtue and rule of law: With an examination of East Asian and Chinese traditional legal culture. *Social Sciences in China, 6.*
15. Nonet, P., & Selznick, P. (1994). *Law and society in transition* (p. 107). China University of Political Science and Law Press.
16. Dejia, L. (2016). *The innovative value of Confucian 'rule of virtue' thought in social governance. Theory and Reform, 1.*
17. Qing, J. (1991). From heart-nature Confucianism to political Confucianism: On another developmental path for contemporary new Confucianism. *Journal of Shenzhen University (Humanities & Social Sciences Edition), 1.*
18. Fasheng, Z. (2016). The misguided path of political Confucianism: The case of Jiang Qing. *Exploration and Free Views, 4.*
19. Qichao, L. (2004). *History of pre-Qin political thought* (p. 98). Tianjin Ancient Books Publishing House.

www.ingramcontent.com/pod-product-compliance
Ingram Content Group UK Ltd.
Pitfield, Milton Keynes, MK11 3LW, UK
UKHW020753220926
475829UK00004BA/93

* 9 7 8 9 8 1 9 5 9 0 5 8 2 *